The Mind and Art of Evelyn Waugh

The Mind and Art of Evelyn Waugh

Binay Kumar Sinha

PUBLISHERS & DISTRIBUTORS (P) LTD

Published by

PUBLISHERS & DISTRIBUTORS (P) LTD

7/22, Ansari Road, Darya Ganj, New Delhi-110002
Phones : +91-11-40775252, 23273880, 23275880, 23280451
Fax : +91-11-23285873
Web : www.atlanticbooks.com
E-mail : orders@atlanticbooks.com

Branch Office
5, Nallathambi Street, Wallajah Road, Chennai-600002
Phones : +91-44-64611085, 32413319
E-mail : chennai@atlanticbooks.com

Printed in India at Nice Printing Press, A-33/3A, Site-IV, Industrial Area, Sahibabad, Ghaziabad, U.P.

Preface

Evelyn Waugh, a British writer of novels, biographies and travel books was born and brought up in the shadow of the First and Second World War. In his work he mirrors his time's political, moral, social, literary, and intellectual impact on the sense and sensibility of the age. He also writes comedy establishing a link between romanticism and realism in view of the tangled web of controversy over the art of fiction-writing generated by the master-builders of fiction like Virginia Woolf, D.H. Lawrence, and James Joyce on the one hand, and Aldous Huxley, C.P. Snow, and Graham Greene on the other.

The book studies how Waugh's writings bear the influences of socio-political changes that took place during the first half of twentieth century, particularly due to two World Wars, and the intellectual and literary crises of large magnitude that occurred as a result. The traditional way of writing as adopted by Waugh has been discussed.

An author can be assessed properly from the critical opinions his work elicits. An exclusive chapter has been devoted to critical opinions on Waugh, such as those of Frederick J. Stopp, Anthony Burgess, Patricia Corr, and A.A. De Vitis. The book also studies Waugh as a man which is deemed essential to judge his mind and art in a clear perspective. But since such a study is difficult without a careful look at his biographical data, a bio-critical method has been used to get a peep into his personality. The purpose is to know Waugh's bent of mind, which if properly analyzed, seeks to search for meaning and purpose in every phenomenon of life. A careful study of his mind also makes us aware of his inquisitive disposition restlessly probing the mystery of social, political, moral and intellectual questions about human life.

The writing career of Evelyn Waugh has been divided into three phases. Each phase has been discussed in a separate chapter to present a focused study of his works belonging to the respective phase. Like all other important writers of his time, Waugh too has his own points of view without knowing which it is difficult to form a fairly correct assessment of his mind and art. The book includes an analysis of his points of view as reflected in his work. Some concrete points from his works have been taken up to present them by way of conclusion.

The book is rich with references from the text. Besides acknowledging the sources from which the pertinent ideas have been taken to develop each chapter in the form of direct references and notes, there is Select Bibliography at the end for enhanced reading. The book will be useful for the students and teachers of English literature, particularly fiction, and researchers in these fields.

Binay Kumar Sinha

Acknowledgements

I feel indebted first and foremost to my supervisor, Dr. S.N. Prasad of the University of Ranchi who has been my mentor and guide throughout. Had I not been getting his care and inspiration, I just could not have managed to accomplish this work. My thanks are also due to the National Library, Calcutta, The British Council Library, Calcutta and most of my colleagues in the college who have always been a source of encouragement to me in the accomplishment of this work.

I shall be failing in my duty if I do not particularly thank Principal Sri Mangal Dubey and Dr. R.N. Jha, Head of the P.G. Deptt. of English, Ranchi University, without whose constant cooperation I probably could not have been able to take up this work.

I am also thankful to my wife, Bela Sinha for her encouragement.

Binay Kumar Sinha

Contents

1 CHAPTER

Introduction

The present book aims at a concentrated study of the mind and art of Evelyn Waugh in the light of the mutation in the sense and sensibility of the present age. Obviously, this dissertation cannot claim to be looked upon as the last word on Waugh's works; yet an endeavour has to be made to understand Waugh's mind having its cumulative effect on his art. In this effort, it should be of no small significance to take into account the various opinions of critics and scholars on Waugh. Another equally helpful aspect of the present scheme would be to relate the author under study to his backgrounds—literary as well as others, namely intellectual, social and political. This hindsight should go a long way in assisting us in the ambitious exploration of a fairly wide coverage comprising the mind and art of Waugh. The second chapter highlights this very aspect of the thesis with a view to mapping out a total and composite background.

Next in order of importance is the task of studying Waugh the man with such thoroughness as should make it absolutely necessary that a whole chapter is devoted to a close study of the man. But here it must be remembered that neither the basic purpose nor the basic structure of the thesis would justify a straightforward biography. The astounding features have to be picked out from a plethora of data with a clear plan to connect the formative phase with the phase of fruition.

This done, it would be proper to turn to the texts in order to see once again the creator in the length and breadth of his creation. A critical discussion of his novels right from his early phase down to the end will be made with a view to having a clear grasp of the development of his art. For this a separate discussion of each phase of his artistic career—early, middle and the end should be made with every care to underline in clear terms the points of growth. On the basis of this discussion the overall importance of characterisation in the framework of his fiction must needs be emphasised. It may also be pointed out as unambiguously as possible that Waugh the novelist just does not fight shy of going back to and making an uninhibited use of the old, beaten track of novel-writing of the eighteenth century. Indeed, this has perhaps helped him convey his ideas to his readers with utmost clarity, and in this achievement, his wit and humour have been chiefly instrumental.

Finally, it may be mentioned that so much has been made of a commonplace criticism of Waugh—the fact that there is much in his work that is downright 'trivial'. Now this is provoking enough; at least it has provoked me just enough to examine the charge of the wider perspective of Waugh's entire work. This is an integral part of my plan to refute the charge of frivolity as a baseless one on the grounds of the artistic devices adopted by Evelyn Waugh.

It should always be kept in our view that Evelyn Waugh is first and foremost a novelist whose art of writing lies in concealing his art. On this ground one should assume that he seldom exposes himself as to whether he writes satire or comedy. There is hardly any writer who is not sarcastic and comic at places and this is true of Waugh as well. But this alone would never justify an allegation that Waugh does not write anything except satire and comedy; at least, this is not expected of a responsible critic. No doubt, as a writer of fiction, Waugh deals with the human world and as such characters will form a nucleus of his art and artifice. Naturally one must stress the primary importance of characters in his fiction which places him easily in the rank of the eighteenth-century novelists like Henry Fielding and Defoe on the one hand and Charles Dickens and Jane Austen and George Eliot on the other in the later phases of the history of fiction. Also, this may help one find Waugh a fairly respectable place in the great tradition of the English novel.

2

CHAPTER

Background of Evelyn Waugh—Social, Political, Moral, Literary and Intellectual

It is difficult to assess the mind and art of Evelyn Waugh without making a minute study of the background he was born to. Waugh was born in 1903 and brought up in the shadow of the first and second world wars that ushered in their trail social, political, moral, intellectual and literary crises of great magnitude. His writings as such seem to bear the influences of these changes to a considerable extent. He is very much in tune with the spirit of his time and it really becomes difficult to judge him in true colours without having a 'historical sense' of the period he belongs to. In his attitudes, impressions and reactions, he is a true artist who seriously deplores the irreparable loss of the primal age of innocense in the wake of the industrial revolution. In his famous autobiography, *A Little Learning*, Waugh seems to be very regretfully referring to the obliteration of villages in the following manner when he writes:

> More than once already in the preceding pages mention has been made of the obliteration of English villages. The process is notorious and inevitable. Expostulation is futile, lament tedious. This is part of the cyclorama of spoliation which surrounded all English experience in this century and any understanding of the past (which presumably is the motive for reading a book such as this) must be incomplete

> unless this huge deprivation of the quiet pleasures of the eye is accepted as a dominant condition, sometimes making for impotent resentment, sometimes for more sentimental apathy, sometimes poisoning love of country and of neighbours. To have been born into a world of beauty and to die amid ugliness is the common fate of all us exiles.[1]

Obviously, this should reflect the reaction of not Waugh alone but of the European sensibility as a whole. It seems as if by and large all writers found themselves face to face with a challenge to their art and sensibility. D.H. Lawrence too like Waugh seems to have seriously deplored the loss of paradisal bliss in the extinction of the agricultural way of life that had stood in his eyes for some definite ideal and significance. This sort of idealisation of rural values on their part aims without doubt at the spiritual loss during the later years of the nineteenth century. In his well-known as well as well-timed novel *Kangaroo*, Lawrence describes the collapse of the pre-industrial values in the following observation which corroborates his sad reaction:

> It was in 1915 the old world had changed. In the winter 1915-16 the spirit of the old London collapsed, the city in some way perished, perished from being the heart of the world, and became a vortex of broken passions, lusts, hopes, fears, and horrors. The integrity of London collapsed and the genuine debasement began, the unspeakable baseness of the public voice, the reign of that bloated ignominy, John Bull....[2]

A minute scrutiny of the passage, quoted above, would suggest that a spirit of distintegration had invaded the very consciousness of the age in almost all spheres of life. In view of this background of cultural deterioration, the loss of the world of art and culture would appear to be incalculable. Psychologically speaking, it was the question of adjustment to the then spirit of the age that became prominent once for all in the eyes of artists. It seemed as if they felt discouraged to write anything as such. The reaction was too disappointing indeed to allow them to feel the urge of creative writing as the old-fashioned world—their usual theme of writing had disappeared completely. Fed up with the abrupt emergence of this peculiar phase in human civilisation, E.M. Forster had almost stopped writing novels for a pretty long time. The following observation of his explains this statement quite clearly:

> ...I think one of the reasons why I stopped writing novels is that the social aspect of the world changed so much. I had been accustomed to write about the old-fashioned world with its homes and its family life and its comparative peace. All that went, and though I can think about the new world I cannot put it into fiction.[3]

In the light of this disappointing reaction of E.M. Forster to the aspects of his age, it becomes undoubtedly clear that the world of writers faced a grim challenge to the conscience of art and culture. This age was thus an age of crisis which forced the writers to revaluate and reassess the worth and ideal of their time. G.H. Bantock's observation in this context is noteworthy when he asserts:

> The pervasive feeling certainly is that any material gain must be balanced against a perceptible spiritual loss, and it is the spiritual loss which has received the literary attention, even though one realises in saying so that the division itself over simplifies the situation.[4]

The underlying spirit of the time then was that of division, disintegration and chaos. It seemed as if any literary critic who sought to probe the consciousness of the times could afford to ignore this at his own risk.

However, this must be noted here that there were several responsible factors behind this prevailing spirit of chaos and disintegration. The two disastrous world wars for example had left their inescapable influences on the sense and sensibility of writers and critics alike. Undoubtedly, these wars had challenged once for all the very conventional values of human life and left their undeniable impact consequently upon the social and political milieu of the then period. To quote Walter Allen in this connection:

> After the first world war the age that had ended in July 1914 seemed as remote as the far side of the moon. The war split

> the landscape of time like an enormous natural catastrophe, obliterating long-established boundaries, blowing sky-high landmarks that for years had been taken for granted. It lay like an unbridgeable chasm between the present and the past, so that present and past seemed almost laughably different in kind. It set a gulf between the young who had fought it and the old who had stayed at home. What had seemed certainties, all the assumptions nurtured in Britain by a hundred years of virtual peace, during which wars were fought either by foreigners or, if the British were involved, by small professional armies on the peripheries of empire, were exposed as illusions.[5]

Walter Allen has explained fairly convincingly the disastrous effects of world wars which put writers in a direct confrontation with the challenging forces of time. As a consequence of these vital changes, it really became difficult for them to appreciate their time in the true sense. As such the present and the past both looked quite different in kind and the existing assumptions—social, political, moral and intellectual were shattered to pieces altogether. Writers in the wake of such vital changes felt that they had no alternative to re-examining and revaluating their period in the light of the dominating forces of time. They noticed in no time that the old order had changed yielding place to the new.

Not merely that, the advancement of modern science had also no less powerful impact upon the artistic sensibility of the time. A.C. Ward in the following observation of his records this sharp change in sensibility in this manner:

> Little more than half a century separated the end of Queen Victoria's reign from the beginning of Elizabeth II's, yet in that first fifty years of the twentieth century the human race moved faster forward and backward—than during perhaps fifty generations in the past. Man's growing mastery of the physical world and material resources is a story of ever-accelerating progress accompanied in its later phases by an un-precedented moral and spiritual relapse. Progress and regress both are fruits in the Scientific Revolution which has been the outstanding feature of this century.[6]

A.C. Ward thus refers to the unprecedented moral and spiritual relapse which was the outcome of the Scientific Revolution. The implication is that the scientific revolution had completely changed the outlook of the new generation, as a result of which the Victorian ethos collapsed altogether. The Faustian urge for more and more knowledge which in its forward march proved to be a curse rather than a blessing in the interest of mankind as a whole, forced the men and women of the twentieth century to look back upon the Victorian age with an eye of disdain. They pooh-poohed their ideology, their established way of life in the name of the Scientific Revolution which was not merely a revolution in the human ingenuity, e.g. the inventions of speedy motorcars and engines of destruction, but also a revolution in the morals and manners of their time. The two worlds thus seemed to be diametrically opposed to each other in their impressions of and attitudes to their culture. A.C. Ward illustrates this point further:

> The old certainties were certainties no longer, everything was held to be open to question. Standards of artistic craftsmanship and of aesthetic appreciation began to change fundamentally. What the Victorians had considered beautiful their children and grandchildren thought hideous.[7]

And again:

> The treasured bric-a-brac of Victorian mantleshelves and whatnots was thrown into Edwardian and Georgian dustbins, though before the reign of George V. was out many of the rejects had become 'antiques' and collectors' pieces: wholesale destruction had conferred the glamour of rarity upon objects formerly distinguished only as evidence of bad tests.[8]

These quotes should indicate a radical change in the criterion of the judgement of the so-called values of life and record how the twentieth-century universe seemed astonishingly different from that of the preceding century. Ward has pointed out how the Gothic architecture seemed to have toppled down in the wake of the Scientific Revolution and from its debris did emerge a world of terror and repulsive beauty. It appears that the mere test of human knowledge lay in pecuniary gains, the result of which was a kind of Midas touch that connected everything into matter or in terms of T.S. Eliot "a heap of broken images." The eyes, it thus appears, that saw the universe affected by the touch and vanish of science, faced a glaring phenomenon all around. The Victorian faith thus crumbled into pieces; the abyss seemed to be gaping wide beneath one's feet. The idols of the Victorian temple were thus desecrated with the impious touch of the man of the twentieth century and the world of permanence consequently suffered a hard blow. Indeed nothing seemed to escape the questioning eyes of the twentieth-century man as a result of this change in outlook which was to quote Ward again, "due to the growth of a restless desire to probe and question.... Bernard Shaw, foremost among the heralds of change, attacked with vigour the 'old superstition of religion' and the 'new superstition' of science not because in his view, every dogma is a superstition until it has been personally examined and consciously accepted by the individual believer. Question/ Examine/Test—these were the watchwords of his creed."[9]

Obviously, the Victorian temper of accepting anything and everything on its face value without any voice of dissent met with a permanent burial and the twentieth-century man applied his penetrating intellect to test and examine everything thoroughly. The Home, the Constitution, the Empire, the Christian religion—each of these which had been taken as final revelations were subject to discussion and most surprisingly everything seemed to be in the eternal flow in the light of the inquiring spirit of the age. Observed in this light, the twentieth century seemed to be an age of re-examination, revaluation, re-assessment and re-adjustment, although the 'eternal flow of things' as referred to by H.G. Wells didn't allow the men and women of the time to rest even for a single moment at one particular pace of human progress.

The year 1900 thus (historically speaking) begins as an age of unprecedented change. R.A. Scott James also has not failed to notice the sweeping changes brought about by the currents and cross-currents of the time when he attempts a stock-taking of the whole situation.

> To me, looking back, the year 1900 really does stand out as a turning point.... It was the beginning of the supremacy of the middle classes and middle class standards of thought and writing. The Fabian Society, an organisation of intellectuals preaching doctrinaire Socialism under the leadership of Sidney Webb and Bernard Shaw had already established itself and the Labour Party was starting its career as a political body led by Keir Hardie and Ramsoy Mac Donald.[10]

Such minute details as mentioned above give a correct insight into the inquiring spirit of the age. Not only that, it provides us as with a clear-cut grasp of the upsurge of humanism that stressed the need of a serious probe into the inquiring spirit of the time and made the people re-examine all the aspects of life—social, political, moral, intellectual and literary.

It must, however, be noted here in this context that outwardly the two ages—the end of the Victorian age and the beginning of the twentieth century might appear identical in their questioning spirit, their reaction to the social milieu with all their new horizons of thoughts and ideas, but in fact they are poles apart from each other.

The sense of revolt against the preceding ages is a common phenomenon in every age and the old order changes yielding place to the new but what marks the difference and intrinsic divergence of the twentieth-century man from that of his Victorian counterpart is his being far more critical, ratiocinative, incredulous, and yet confident than the latter. The notion of this over-confidence and undue hair-splitting of almost all the issues consequently results in a total lack of stability, permanence and concentration. Speed as a result of such attitudes becomes a watchword which forces his fast-moving intellect to re-examine, re-assess and re-fashion the universe. The spectacles of science as such press him to re-examine the universe; the study of moral science perplexes him in re-assessing the values of the time and thus in the light of the changes wrought by the two world wars, everywhere his vision perplexes and retardes him. It seems as if what he has just seen deceives him immediately and forces him to re-examine it. His meandering vision thus does not allow him to feel at rest, as a result of which he ever remains unsatiated. The Faustian urge to know thus more and more gives him little rest. No ideal as such appears to be pleasing and satisfying to him; everything is seen to be in the cobweb of illusion and scepticism. The doubter doubts himself first of all, and while disbelieving himself he disbelieves everything he sees, hears and understands. Both the ages as such—the twentieth century and the Victorian age need by no means be confused and considered as synonymous in their attitudes to life and the trends of charges in thoughts and ideals. Broadly speaking, the ideal of the former (the Victorian) is to be critical of the ideals of society whereas the ideal of the latter (the Edwardians) is to refute everything and accept nothing as an ideal. "The early twentieth century", writes R.A. Scott James, "had for its characteristic to put everything, in every sphere of life to the question, and secondly in the light of this scepticism, to reform, to reconstruct, to accept the new age as new, and attempt to mould it by conscious, purposeful effort."[11]

The spirit of this constant enquiry into every sphere of life and the tendency to "put everything, in every sphere of life of the question, and to reform and re-construct everything in the light of this scepticism" as mentioned above, appear to have become a common fact hardly to be ignored by a conscientious artist. Undoubtedly, there was a trace of decline and fall in the very set-up and existence of mankind and the question as to how to adjust and appreciate the very nuances of change, had become more important than ever before. The effect of this sudden change was seen in the feelings and thoughts which had animated humanity long before the advance of modern science. The result of this change was a sincere motivation in the world of artists to examine the problems of destiny, conduct and self-hood. Darwin's theory of the Origin of Species propelled mankind to judge the mind and art of this period in a different way as a result of which there remained hardly any field of thinking that was not affected by it. To quote H.V. Routh in this context for a better and more satisfactory explanation of the whole issue:

> This interest caused perplexity and restlessness, because it was two sided culminating in a paradox. On the one hand no

> thoughtful and imaginative reader could accept the physical and biological conclusions, so amply documented from Lyell to Huxley, without admitting that the universe looks like a colossal blunder, that human life on our inhospitable globe is an accident, due to unknown causes which may never be repeated and that this accident has involved more suffering and maladjustment than any other form of evolution; and for certain temperaments the interpretation stops there, ending in stoicism, overwhelming pity or despair. Thomas Hardy, Mark Rutherford, A.E. Housman, and Somerset Maugham are examples. On the other hand, it was equally permissible to admit that Nature was not indeed a system planned by a Divine Architect or Economist, but an experimental force, appallingly wasteful and pitiless, but infinitely resourceful and adaptable, hopelessly un-economical, but irrepressively progressive. Those who faced the evidence fairly and squarely, instead of losing faith in the tradition of human grandeur, might be rewarded with a new romance of self-knowledge, based on scientific truth. The materialists were perhaps not mistaken.[12]

It is perfectly clear that the ruling temper of the time favoured a scientific point of view. The effect was too grave indeed to allow men of letters and ideas to judge the values of their age with the same old standard and concept of moral judgement. Besides, the observers of the then period because of their matter-of-fact approach to their period of transition were termed "materialists" as mentioned above by H.V. Routh. The emergence of such materialists on the literary scene of the time, however, presupposes the existence of a group of spiritualists also to have been present at that time. These two extremes of thought thus seem to have gripped the attention of readers and critics alike.

The post-war world as such in the light of these changes appears to be quite a different generation in itself which in the sudden replacement of old ideas by the new ones, allowed nothing to remain static. The crisis was thus a worldwide one which left its impact on the social, political, moral and intellectual field. It was in one word the question of survival that dominated the mind of artists and critics both. To quote A.A. De Vitis in this context for a satisfactory and convincing verification:

> The nineteenth century left to the twentieth a growing uneasiness in the face of the materialistic advances of science and the rising influence of the middle class. Moral and political ideas succumbed to the influence of Lenin and Marx, and the human personality found itself to the analyses of Jung and Freud. T.S. Eliot detected a death-wish in Western civilization, defined it and set forth the most comprehensive set of symbols for characterising the period of the early years of the century. Few serious thinkers were able to maintain orthodox belief in the face of all this confusion and turmoil.... In the late twenties and early thirties there came a depression following upon the inflation and the make good time of the post-war period. Economic catastrophe was a reality. The early thirties began to bring the threat of still more war. The hopes of Shaw and the Fabians dimmed in the tide of Spanish fascism and German totalitarianism.[13]

This long passage quoted above provides a striking note of mutation in the world of thought current caused by the materialistic advances of science and technology which in the words of A.A. De Vitis forced the writers not to "maintain orthodox belief in the faces of all this confusion". It becomes crystal clear that in the wake of this unprecedented revolution in almost all spheres of life as such writers felt seriously concerned about their fate on this planet. They thus naturally detected a kind of wish for death in view of the irreparable loss to the values of tradition. The ravages of war had thus a profound impact upon the economy of nations that forced them to re-construct and re-furbish their image in the eyes of theirs as well as the world. The political upheaval was such as it became quite difficult for nations to choose any particular political doctrine in the wake of unheard of changes. It was because of this serious change in the political field that the cult of nationalism became more prominent than before as a result of this tremor. The cult of nationalism was thus the corollary of a general cry for personal safety and security. The post-war Europe thus found itself confronted with a variety of perplexing questions and in many cases democracy as a form of government in view of the ravages of war failed to satisfy them. It was on account of this notion that democracy was replaced by dictatorship in various countries notably in Italy, Russia, Germany and Spain barring Britain. England maintained its fundamental stability in the political field in spite of the major crises of the inter-war period such as the General Strike of 1926, the abdication of King Edward VIII in December 1936, as well as the threat of invasion in the earlier part of the Second World War. To quote Grant and Temperley in this context for a thorough realisation of the details:

> It's true that in the period between the two wars the constitution of the British Commonwealth grew notably looser and more flexible. Great Britain alone signed the Pact of Locarno, Canada, Australia, New Zealand and South Africa abstained.... In the age-old struggle between the eternally opposed ideas of liberty and authority the battle has by no means been lost and much of the basis for the hope for the future is to be found in the democracies overseas. The strategic position in this struggle is held by the New World and the growing number of the free states of the Dominions. So long as they survive, the odds against liberty are hardly greater than they were in earlier ages.[14]

The above-mentioned facts should enable one to have a correct insight into the two opposed doctrines fighting for their survival in the changed political set up of the time. It is on account of these factors that an appreciation of the literary sensibility of the time becomes extremely difficult. Bertrand Russell's remarks in this context are quite noteworthy:

> Traditional systems of dogma and traditional codes of conduct have not the hold they formerly had. Men and Women are often in genuine doubt as to what is right and what is wrong, and even as to whether right and wrong are anything more than ancient superstition. When they try to decide such questions for themselves they find them too difficult. They cannot discover any clear purpose of any clear principle by which they should be guided.[15]

Russell in one way is discussing the ideas of his time in a most precise manner touching on the important points having their bearing on the consciousness of the time but he explains it further:

> Stable societies may have principles that, to the outsider, seem absurd. But so long as the societies remain stable their principles are subjectively adequate. That is to say they are accepted by almost everybody unquestioningly, and they make the rules of conduct as clear and precise as those of the minuet or the heroic couplet. Modern life, in the West is not at all like a minuet or a heroic couplet. It is like free verse which only the poet can distinguish from prose.[16]

Bertrand Russell has done well to stress the nuances of change which are too subtle to allow one to conceive them in the right perspective. None but a poet, he writes, could distinguish it from prose on account of the accents and attitudes being quite new in themselves which the connoisseurs of art alone could analyse clearly. The whole civilization as such on the basis of the above statement seems to be on a trial which is quite different in shape and substance from that of Victorianism. Arnold Toynbee's opinion is quite noteworthy in this connection:

> The Western world has become rather suddenly very anxious about its own future, and our anxiety is a natural reaction to the formidableness of ourselves. Our present situation is formidable indeed.[17]

The use of epithets like 'anxiety', 'formidable', 'instability', 'freeverse' leaves little doubt in the mind of critics that it is not easy to define the mind and spirit of the time in this age of transition.

Viewed against this social, political, moral, intellectual and economic background of bewildering diversity confronting the modern man, these conflicting forces of time leave their considerable impact on the technique of writing novels. The myth of a universal human nature as a consequence of such hostile forces seems to have been finally exploded and the modes of behaviour obviously changed. The impact of this change is seen on the form and content of writing. The sense of bewilderment and confusion in appreciating the genres of literature of the period thus becomes quite common. The age appears to be typical in itself and strangely enough, every kind of approach looks original. Every one whether he be a poet, a novelist or a short-story writer, with the stethescope of his vision attempts to feel the heart-beat of his time but his approach is never the same. It is because of this sudden change in sensibility that poetry, novel, drama and other branches of literature assume different forms and shapes. The period as such calls for the need of a fresh scrutiny in every branch and the old tools of judgement fail to grasp the current spirit of time. To quote A.J.J. Ratcliff in this context for a vivid perception of the prevailing spirit of the times.

> The years following the war of 1914-18 were in England, as elsewhere, a time of heart-searching; the accepted world and all its implications seemed to have crumbled into dust, and it became clear that a fresh scrutiny of life must be made and a fresh position established. Some there were who found themselves too baffled and distraught to do anything but shrug their shoulders in a cynical despair. Others took up an attitude of defiance and revolt. Most tried to re-construct their outlook temperately without throwing tradition and authority utterly to the winds, yet without the confident front of their unbroken elders (such as Wells and Shaw). The general result was a stern stock-taking, an uncompromising truth-facing, and a distrust of idealism, sentiment and 'progress.' It was the age of the awkward question and the candid answer.[18]

Being thus an age of 'awkward question' and 'stern stock-taking' the answer had to be candid in nature. It was an awkward age because of the multitudinous variety of thoughts, and ideas governing the consciousness of the time. Besides, the attitude of defiance and distrust is accompanied with a sense of veneration for the ideals of the past. This sort of ambivalent attitude on the part of artists and critics alike makes the age more and more awkward in nature and calls for a frank and candid answer from a conscientious artist. The richness and variety as such become most important attributes of the literature and art of this transition period. The influences coming from different continents also play their significant role in modifying the growth and structure of the different genres of literature.

The continental influences leave their impact on the art of fiction-writing to a considerable extent. While judging the worth and dignity of the English novel, it therefore becomes natural on the part of literary critic to notice the bearings of foreign writings on the craft of fiction-writing. The effect is so apparent that language and literature both become continental in nature and it offen appears risky to term it English exclusively. Henry James in his delineation of new themes and conventions, contrary to the spirit of the Victorian era, becomes a dominating force to be reckoned with. It is on account of such factors that George Sampson in his famous book *The Concise Combridge History of English Literature* refers very gladly to the emergence of the cosmopolitan ideas in the literary scene of the period and is seldom oblivious of the grave impact it seems to have left upon the form and content of novel-writing, and their branches of literature. He writes quite clearly as to how the English-speaking world derives such continental influences spontaneously in the following manner:

> As we arrive in our final chapter, with the groundwork and some of the details already thus prepared, it will come as a surprise to no one that the accent throughout will be upon the world which speaks English, not upon the nation which had the privilege of having spoken and written it in the first place. Prophecy is as dangerous in literary matters as in political, and in this instance they may well be connected, but we are running no great risk of having to eat out our English words when we say that literature in the English langauge is likely to become more and more cosmopolitan the further the twentieth century proceeds towards its own manifest destiny in the twenty first. If the accent of mid-twentieth century English literature is so clearly international, the accent—or the varying accents—of late twentieth century English literature is hereby likely to be less so. The international, cosmopolitan nature of "English literature" meets us now every turn.[19]

It thus becomes abundantly clear on the basis of the observation noted above that the 'international' and 'cosmopolitan' nature of "English literature" draws the attention of every sensitive critic in the evaluation and assessment of the literary spirit of this period. Henry James, the pioneer of modern fiction could be intelligent enough to grasp these new accents and attitudes governing the literary sensibility of his time. The confirmation of this mutation in the sensibility of the time is clearly found in the following statement of Walter Allen when he says:

> By the eighteen-eighties the mutation that had occurred in the novel with George Eliot and Meredith had become dominant. Novelists were conscious of a split in fiction between the old and the new and while significant novels of the older type continued to be written—and still they are—they had more and more the appearance of throwbacks to the past.[20]

Walter Allen thus in the above passage marks the change of sensibility owing to several responsible factors having their impact upon the existing sensibility of the tme; he however supplements himself by quoting Henry James's own views regarding the change in the art of fiction-writing.

> I was lately struck, in reading over many pages of Anthony Trollope, with his want of discretion in this particular. In a digression, a paranthesis or an aside, he concedes to the reader that he and this trusting friend (fiction) are only 'making believe'. He admits that the events he narrates have not really happened, and that he can give his narrative any turn the reader may like best. Such a betrayal of a secred office seems to me, I confess, a terrible crime; it is what I mean by the attitude of apology, and it shocks me every whit as much in Trollope as it would have shocked me in Gibbon or Macaulay.[21]

Henry James substantiates his argument quite candidly that the failure on the part of a writer to portray the events he narrates that have not really happened, is not less than the 'betrayal of a sacred office' a novelist is supposed to undertake in the best interests of the art and the office he holds. The implication is that he does not countenance the sacred office of a novelist being misused by him in any way. He gives a stern rebuke to such a kind of careless and irresponsible craftsman who "is less occupied in looking for the truth than the historian and in doing so it deprives him at a stroke of all his standing room."[22]

James would appear to be the morning star of the new generation of fiction-writers who surveys the task of an artist in the context of the changed set-up of society and calls for a re-assessment and re-interpretation of the truths of life yet unexplored in the history of the novel. The craft of fiction-writing as a result of his clarion call to artists and critics alike assumes a new dimension. His honesy as well as sincerity of approach does not allow the novelist to be a historian but a fine artist instead whose main task is, as it seems, to draw a very convincing and delicate portrait of mankind.

He says: "The only reason for the existence of a novel is that it does attempt to represent life. When it relinquishes this attempt, the same attempt that we see on the canvas of the painter, it will have arrived at a very strange pass. It is not expected of the picture that it will make itself humble in order to be forgiven; and the analogy between the art of the painter and the art of the novelist is complete. Their inspiration is the same, their purpose (allowing for the different quality of the vehicle), is the same, their success is the same. They may learn from each other, they may explain and sustain each other, their cause is the same and the honour of one is the honour of another."[23]

A careful scrutiny of the above passage gives an insight into the association of the art of fiction-writing with the art of painting which must by all means be the ultimate end of an artist while writing fiction. In one way, it is the photographic realism that in his opinion ought to be the ultimate end of the novelist. It is thus the call for refinement and perfection in the art of fiction-writing that becomes the prime concern of a writer of fiction today. The art of fiction-writing becomes a controversial issue, as a result of which the theory of naturalism does not appear to be the same as it was in the preceding century. It is therefore natural on the part of critics to come across the terms like 'impressionism', 'naturalism' and 'realism' which, if looked into minutely, connote the varied shades of realism having their different forms in accordance with the spirit and sensibility of times. Here Allen's observation is very apt.

> Words applied to literary and artistic movements revolutionary in their day have soldom—any precise meaning. They are emotive words, slogans, battle-cries to rouse the faithful. Often, as with the word 'Impressionist' as applied to the French painters of the second half of the nineteenth century, they come into existence quite by chance, as journalistic coinings that are seized upon and given currency as conventional labels. Naturalism, naturalistic are such words. They have certain attributes, but the sum-total of these attributes is not enough truly to describe the work of the great masters of Naturalism-Maupassant and Zola. The very difference between these writers, who as artists are poles apart, is enough to show up the inadequacy of the word as a label. Yet when the attributes are borne in mind, it still has its value to categorize a certain kind of fiction, a kind that, often in an impure state, more or less dominated the writing of the novel throughout Europe and America from the mid-eighties to about 1914.[24]

Here the main implication is that in view of the different categories of fiction-writing, there are varied forms which give full evidence of the different theories of naturalism propounded by different writers today. Modern fiction as such is rich in various ways in so far as the attitudes to life are concerned today. Flaubert, Bernard Shaw, Chekhov, Taine, Emily, Zola, Strindberg and others in spite of being identical in their belief that the function of novel is to present the illusion of reality, differ in the very modes of their presentation of the reality of life today. Flaubert, for instance, maintains that the writer must describe what he detests with utter accuracy and since society must be sure to object to it, heroic honesty. Shaw again in his opinion considers it his sacred duty to expose the falsity of ideals by freeing himself as well as his readers from absurd allegiances. Taine in his analysis seems to be making elaborate and dogmatic effort to represent man as a covergence of the environmental forces rather than as a self-mover and thus rejects the picture of the artist as isolated and godlike, arbitrarily composing autonomous works attaching due weight to the race, the milieu and the moment of history. Zola on the other hand feels like photographing the illusion of reality while Strindberg considers the prime duty of the artist to represent the dynamic character of the individual and society on account of their being dynamic in nature. Thus, Strindberg does not consider human beings as the personifications of fixed traits because of their falling a prey to the forces and circumstances of their time. It is because of this awareness he stresses the representation of his characters being characterless in nature. Evelyn Waugh's fiction does not as such look free from the influences of these writers who help us in understanding his mind and art. Henry James in the light of such bearings does not seem to be wrong, insincere and irresponsible in giving a clarion call to artists and critics alike to re-evaluate and re-assess the art of novel-writing. He thus appears in my opinion to be the first person as a conscientious artist to grasp the current of the changed sensibility of his time. Owing to these responsible factors the modern fiction seldom appears to be the same in nature and spirit, accent and attitude as that of the Victorian age. The failure on the part of a critic to mark this serious change in sensibility is as such sure to lead him to errors of judgement and perception of the whole issue at his command. The English novel of today is as a result of this sharp change in sensibility not as voluminous as it was seen in the preceding centuries. It is the rigorous selection of incident and material that becomes more important than anything today. The need of design and shape is for the first time felt in the case of fiction-writing. The writing of novel becomes thus a conscious and careful pursuit in itself forming a discipline so to say. To quote Walter Allen for a full clarification of this issue:

> The English novel had been like a hold-all into which anything could be stuffed. The one-volume novel imposed upon the novelist the necessity for a much more rigorous selection of incident and material.... It was this, "together with the demands of new reading publics, that led to the breakdown

> of the Victorian novel into the categories of fiction that we know today however we may describe them—the straight novel, the psychological novel, the novel of adventure, the detective novel, the thriller, the woman's romance. Where the very great were concerned this was probably an impoverishment, but the new length of the novel was itself cartainly a powerful aid to those writers like Stevenson, James, George Moore, Conrad, and Bennett, whose view of the novel was of an autonomous work consciously shaped.[25]

It is thus abundantly clear that the design and shape become more important than anything else in the English novel as if the art of fiction-writing were for the first time making an urgent demand for perfection which led the practitioners of modern fiction to decide its fate afresh. Novel writing in its skill then appears to be not less than a beautiful work of embroidery which is the natural result of the scientific approach to modern life and art. Perhaps, it would not be an exaggeration then to accept Henry James as the father of modern fiction. This is really an unforgettable contribution of Henry James to the growth and structure of modern fiction. George Sampson's remarks about his artistic achievement are worthy of appreciation:

> In his work we find a double inheritance: one stemming from Hawthorne and the Puritan ethos of New England, the other from Jane Austen and the later George Eliot. Even James, of course, great as he is in many ways, was not heir to all the ages of the English and American novel. Although in his autobiographical sketches he writes reverently and movingly of the creator of Copperfield and gives him the name of Master with equal conviction of capital initial to George Eliot herself—he had had the privilege of meeting both Masters personally—what we may loosely call the "outdoor" or "masculine" tradition in the British novel, from Defore, Fielding and Smollett to Scott and Dickens, affects his work much less specifically than the "drawing-room" of "feminine" tradition of Richardson, Jane Austen and certain chapters in the later George Eliot. Nor is there much connection, save in theme, so differently handled, of "innocents abroad", between James and that more

> consciously American tradition we have been discussing, whose masterpiece is Huckleberry Finn, and which seems to some American critics to be the only genuine native tradition, James in this view being a European or a cosmopolitan novelist rather than an American and the influence on him of Balzac, Flaubert and Turgenev being stressed. "The historian of fine consciences" was the tribute of that other cosmopolitan novelist, Joseph Conrad, and there is little to add or detract from that characteristically just appreciation.[26]

On the basis of the above observation, it becomes quite clear as to how Henry James's art of fiction-writing is the outcome of varied foreign influences. His outlook is cosmopolitan and it is quite natural on the part of sensitive critics to trace the impact of such bearings on his sense and sensibility. Balzac, Flaubert and Turgenev on the one hand form an international character of his fiction and Defoe, Jane Austen and George Eliot give a native hue to his art on the other. His fiction on account of a fine blending of both these factors assumes a psychological character and a keen interest into the mental recesses of mankind becomes consequently a matter of prime concern to artists, especially in the field of fiction-writing. Henry James gives rise to a new brand of naturalism which seems to pre-occupy itself with the inner working of human nature. William James' theory of the "stream of consciousness" leaves an unforgettable imprint on his sensibility as a result of which he appears to have been the first conscious artist to introduce this new phenomenon of human nature in fiction-writing. It is because of the introduction of this new element in fiction-writing that Virginia Woolf wastes no time at all in awakening the world of artists to "look within" and examine the mind that receives myriad impressions—trival, fantastic, evanescent, or engraved with the sharpness of steel.[27] R.A. Scott James too does not fail to notice this new impulse behind the spirit of fiction-writing when he writes how the story of naturalism of the preceding century had completely failed in the delineation of human nature:

> It had exhibited the chemistry of social revolution, and individual reaction to change. But it had not yet carried the

revolution into the mind itself.... In the next phase the conflict was to take place inside the individual mind, the revolution was to be staged in the mysterious recess of the soul; the hidden parts of the conscious or even the unconscious were to be dragged into the open, and the readjustment, if any were possible, was to be made within the privacies of the percipient or suffering mind.[28]

A careful scrutiny of the above passage should help us get at this new brand of naturalism in shape and substance, form and content, matter and spirit which made an artist aware of a new reality of human life hardly discovered before. The art of fiction-writing is thus found treading a new path of progress in the delineation of human nature which has had always been the subject of perennial inspiration to writers in all ages. As a result of this curious change in human sensibility, Virginia Woolf, while scrutinising the prevailing spirit of the age, found herself quite dissatisfied with the conventional mode of fiction-writing and felt compelled to write her provocative views dealing with the materials of fiction which seem to have undergone a sea change:

The proper stuff of fiction does not exist, everything is the proper stuff of fiction; every feeling, every thought; every quality of brain and spirit drawn upon; no perception comes amiss. And if we can imagine the art of fiction come alive and stand in our midst, she would undoubetedly bid us break her and bully her, for so her youth is renewed and her sovereignty assured.[29]

Virginia Woolf's aesthelic sense thus develops out of her psychological insight into the innermost consciousness of this period of transition which gives equal importance to "every feeling" 'every thought' on account of no perception coming amiss. In her famous critical essay "Modern Fiction" she seems to have very modestly explained the failures of artists like Mr. Wells, Mr. Bennett, and Mr. Galsworthy who in her opinion are worthy to be known as 'materialists' because of their pre-occupation with the gross things of life. She does not concieve the reality of life like them and pooh-poohs them in the following way when she further explains her view to justify her stand:

> If we fasten, then, one label on all these books, on which is one word materialists, we mean by it that they spend immense skill and immense industry making the trival and the transitory appear the true and the enduring.[30]

Virginia Woolf stresses the importance of the voyage within rather than the voyage without which becomes as a result of the new bearings and influences on the art of creative writing the sole concern of the writers of the present generation. Judged in the light of her above statement Wells, Arnold Bennelt and Galsworthy would appear to have failed to grasp the thought current of this period and hence worthy to be called materialists. The theory of their naturalism does not seem to be fitting in with the current existence of reality which must needs be spiritual in nature. The Freudian theory of psycho-analysis seems to be a very responsible factor behind this consciousness in this context. Philip Rahv's arguments in this respect deserve their mention for a full clarification of the causes of failure of the theory of naturalism of the preceding century when he holds:

> The point is that this scientific bias of naturalism was historically productive of contradictory results. Its effect was certainly depressive in so far as it brought mechanistic notions and procedures into writing....[31]

And again:

> This means that it has lost the power to cope with the ever-growing element of the problematical in modern life which is precisely the element that is magnetising the imagination of the true artists of our epoch. Such artists are no longer content merely to question particular habits or situations or even institutions, it is reality itself which they bring into question. Reality to them is like that "open wound" of which Kierkeegard speaks in his journal: "A healthy open wound; sometimes it is healthier to keep a wound open; sometimes it is worse when it closes".[32]

Philip Rahv is interested in the interior vision the correct recognition of which becomes the main task of a true artist. This is why, he maintains with confidence that the writers' task is to reveal in the true sense of the term the reality of human life which is the interior world of mankind. The name of D.H. Lawrence under the stress of such influences deserves its mention in this context who in his fiction seems to be treading the uncharted territory of human consciousness which has always been a puzzle to the connoiseurs of art. In Lawrence's view, the chief pre-occupation of a writer is to probe the very substratum of one's personality as a result of which he is focussing into the mystery of sexual life also which in his opinion assumes a special significance in itself. Like Kierkeegard he appears to be catching the cause of 'a healthy open wound' as noted above. In the following observation, he is aiming at this new awareness of thought emerging in the realm of modern fiction:

> You must'nt look in my novel for the old stable ego of character. There is another ego, according to whose action the individual is un-recognisable, and passes through, as it were allotropic states which it needs a deeper sense than any we've been used to exercise, to discover-states of the same simple element of carbon. The ordinary novelist would trace the history of the diamond—but I say, Diamond, what! This is Carbon! And my diamond might be coal or soot, and my theme is carbon.[33]

Lawrence's talk of 'another ego' according to whose action the invidividual is unrecognisable might be termed spiritual in essence and spirit, and this distinguishes him from Wells, Bennett and Galsworthy—the so-called 'materialists' in the opinion of Virginia Woolf. Such an attitude of life seems to be the direct consequence of the spirit of individualism that invaded the consciousness of art after the two world wars prompting man to take refuge into a private universe of his own in view of the values of life having become totally unstable. It is not only Lawrence who countenances the spiritual bent of mind probing the very sub-stratum of human personality but James Joyce too who does not fail to notice the significance of the interior world of art and culture. In employing the 'stream of consciousness' technique he too aims at this new phenomenon of reality resulting in the wonderful creation of works of art like *Ulysses*, *The Portrait of a Young Man* and others.

The twenties as such stands before our eyes as a decade of splendid achievement in the art of fiction-writing. It appears as if for the first time the art of fiction-writing were gaining in depth and analysis of human nature providing the writers with a blissful awareness of the innermost chamber of human consciousness. In the eyes of such writers, the outside world in spite of its bric-a-brac appears to be nothing but the replica of the inner world of an artist. To quote Graham Hough in this context for a full confirmation of this view:

> Then, sometime in the nineteen-twenties, all changed, changed utterly. A whole new literary movement burst upon us. It had to be absorbed and assimilated.... Peaks arose in unexpected places.... The intricacies of Joycean composition required us to look at prose-writing in a new way, with far clear attention to verbal texture and imagery. Henry James's criticism of the novel began to percolate, and we were persuaded to see the novel in terms of an almost musical structure and organisation. Bliss was it in that dawn to be alive, and to be young was very heaven—for it seemed that literary study had got out of the pedants, the professors, and the historians and had entered into a new pact with the creative imagination. "I say" "seemed", for in fact this sense of a new freedom was partly illusory. The fact is a literary revolution was in full swing....[34]

Graham Hough thus judged on the basis of the above observation would appear to be presenting before us a certificate of the art and artifice of these writers but at the same time not feeling oblivious of "a new freedom" being "illusory" in nature. The use of the word "illusory" seems to be full of meanings in this context because of his indirect hint so to say at the movement likely to peter out too soon as it delinked itself from the layman's reality of life with his day-to-day problems. As a matter of fact, the craft of fiction-writing seemed to be the pursuit of a coterie and kept itself confined to a handful of writers enjoying bliss in their own world of ignorance. Arnold Kettle's minute observation in this context explains very convincingly the case of this inner vision in the following words when he holds:

> Writers who feel unable to come to terms with the world at large tend to retreat into the only corner they can feel reasonably sure of their own spiritual predicament and that of a few people like themselves. Hence, the tendency of the twentieth century middle-class writers either to turn it into himself and become entirely involved in his own neuroses or else to confine himself to an exceedingly narrow world in which he happens to feel at home.[35]

The formation of a private universe owing to a sense of despair and alienation being the governing consciousness of the time is worth-recording here for the correct evaluation of art and literature of this period. The fate of the novel thus seems to be decided by a group of serious practitioners in the twenties who at the instance of Henry James feel much more interested in probing into the sanctuary of human self than any other thing in the study of human nature.

However, the twenties died of its own excesses but occupied a niche in the history of English novel. It was a remarkable period in view of the standardisation of English literature as a whole but unfortunately it suffered from a serious flaw of its being far away from the taste of the common reader which failed to appreciate it in the real sense of the term. David Daiches illustrates the enduring value of this period in the following way when he writes:

> In the matter of literary technique the 1920s proved to be one of the most fruitful periods in the whole history of English literature. In fiction, the so-called 'stream of consciousness' method was born, matured and moved to its decline within this single decade. In poetry the revolution wrought by Pound and Eliot and the later Yeats, by the new influence of the twentieth century metaphysical and of Hopkins, changed the poetic map of the century. As far as technique goes, the period since has been one of consolidation. Nothing so redically new in technique as Eliot's *The Waste Land* has appeared since, nor have later novelists ventured as far in technical innovation as Joyce did in *Ulysses* and *Finnegans Wake* (the latter though published in 1939, was largely written in and belongs in spirit to the 1920s).[36]

The passage quoted above explains in the clearest possible words the fertility of the twenties in the field of English literature as a whole as a result of the splendid achievements of craftsman like Virginia Woolf, D.H. Lawrence and James Joyce. The reputation of these writers in the estimation of the general public, however, could not last for a long period due to their narrow appeal to the reading public. Not merely that, either, as it seems to me, they appeared too tough in the eyes of common people to truly appreciate them or too narrow to be a source of permanent inspiration to the future generation of writers. Whatever the cause of the downfall, the twenties had had its day and later met with a sharp reaction as almost all movements seem to be faced with after a temporary phase of growth and prosperity. This reaction came as a result of the writings of some writers like Aldous Huxley, George Orwell, Graham Greene, Evelyn Waugh and C.P. Snow who took a different bias in writing fiction from those of Virginia Woolf, D.H. Lawrence and James Joyce. The theory of naturalism at the hands of such practitioners of fiction took a backward direction and sought to take refuge in the conventional mode of fiction-writing. As a result of such reaction, the old craftsmen in the field of fiction-writing like Defoe, Henry Fielding, Jane Austen, Dickens and George Eliot became their supreme examples of creative writing and they followed their footprints quite devotedly and sincerely. They tried to be as simple and unambiguous as they could be in drawing the portrait of life. It seems as if these writers felt this thing very sincerely that technical innovation in itself was not enough and as such there was an indispensable need to portray society as it was not as it appreared to be in the cloistered shell of their imagination. Also they felt as if the principal task of a novelist were to present a sound analysis of moral, social, political and intellectual problems of their time, which in the wake of the tremendous social change brought about by the post-Versailles society of England needed a faithful and convincing picture of the crisis in the language of the common mass. The twenties in its later phase of literary development thus seems to have undergone a sudden change in the art of presenting the picture of life. Sean O' Faolain points out this curious shift in the technique of fiction-writing due to the sudden overlapping of the twenties into the thirties extolling the importance of the twenties at the same time from the literary point of view:

> I suppose it is fair to say that everybody now recognises that it would be absurd to apply such terms as feckless or irresponsible to a period that produced such writers as Mrs. Woolf, Elizabeth Bowen, Aldous Huxley, Graham Greene, Ernest Hemingway, William Faulkner and Evelyn Waugh—the writers dealt with in this book—all of whom are now-a-days taken seriously, and with one or two possible exceptions, better left unnamed considered quite respectable. And this is to make no mention of writers whom even the period regarded as wholly traditional. Besides, to form a complete literary image of the time the generation must be allowed to overlap. D.H. Lawrence, John Cowper, Powys, Joyce, Yeats, Lytton, Strachey, Somerset Maugham, were all writing at the top of their form in the twenties. To leave these out because they were of an earlier generation would be to form a very squint-eyed picture of the decade. Furthermore, thus overlapping of the generations is crucial for a reason apart altogether from literary figures; which is that tradition can sturdily persist behind all appearances of outward change.[37]

In the above statement, Sean O' Faolain traces out the glorious achievement of the twenties but underlines the value of tradition persisting behind the writings of the artists of this period. By scrutinising the thought-currents of this period thus one comes across conveniently speaking two bands of writers in the later part of the twenties who may be termed in George Sampson's view 'novelists of ideas' and the 'novelists of artistic value'. The thirties thus in the development of the art of fiction-writing appears meaningful and thought-provoking on account of its reactionary attitude to the artistic approach of the twenties. Sean O' Faolain extols the importance of tradition underlying the writings of all no doubt but these writers like Evelyn Waugh, C.P. Snow, Graham Greene and Aldou Huxley deal with the day-to-day ideas of life more intelligently and carefully than the writers like Mrs. Woolf, D.H. Lawrence and James Joyce dealing with the subtle and unconscious world of mankind. Once again, the choice between the Romantic and the Realistic approach to life becomes a question of considerable importance and in the art of fiction-writing of the thirties the leanings and tendencies appear to be in favour of the realistic approach to life and art. It is because of such attitudes to life and art that George Sampson in course of the historical analysis of the trends of writing holds:

> Nor can there be any rigid distinction between what is commonly called "the novel of ideas", as written by such novelists as Wells and Aldous Huxley, and the novel of more artistic value such as those we have mentioned. We rarely have a contrast as clear as that between Peacock and Jane Austen or between Wells and Henry James. Most often it is a question of degree, not of absolute distinction, "Congenital" novelists—as Huxley well calls them—like Forster and Lawrence being also men of ideas, and novelists of ideas like Wells and Huxley sometimes approaching close to the novel conceived as a work of art.[38]

George Sampson has referred to the novelists of ideas and of artistic value just because of the two sorts of leanings prevailing in the world of fiction-writing. He has, however, warned against making any kind of absolute distinction between the two classes of writers because of the intermixture and happy blending of romance and realism being present very often in their writings. To quote him further:

> The distinction we make in this chapter-taking first the "Congenital" novelists from Conrad to Cary, afterwards the novelists of ideas from Wells to Orwell—is therefore for purposes of convenience mainly one of those necessary abbreviations or approximations to truth (like "influences", "movements" and so forth) without which literary history, at any rate in a small compass, could scarcely be written.[39]

It thus becomes perfectly clear that the distinction between the two classes of writers as mentioned above, is meant not in an absolute sense but for one's convenience only. The terms 'congenital' and 'novel of ideas' as borrowed by George Sampson from Huxley in the course of his historical analysis of the current thoughts and ideas are the "necessary abbreviations" or "approximations to truth" only, used with a view to creating a sort of convenience in the mind of readers to understand the trends of writing from time to time. An absolute distinction is quite fatal and misleading in the discussion of such delicate issues. Ideas are without doubt the germs of creative writing in all cases whether a novelist were writing a novel of ideas or artistic value. However, this must be borne in mind in this context that ideas always take their shape in accordance with the individual vision of an artist which might be romantic and realistic both at the same time. Virginia Woolf herself has stated clearly and comprehensively as to how 'everything is the proper stuff of fiction' and 'no perception comes amiss'. Her humble submissions thus does not allow a conscientious writer to adopt any narrow and insular view on such delicate issues. If any perception can be the subject-matter of fiction it would then be suicidal in spirit on the part of a critic to make any such absolute distinction. On the strength of this argument George Sampson would appear to be quite reasonable in his views when he warns us against creating a distinction in any absolute sense. The labels like 'congenital' and 'novel of ideas' are therefore meant for our convenience to understand the spirit of writing only. It's true that the twenties was the decade of originality but there is no guarantee of the decade surviving in the same spirit even in the thirties. It therefore becomes essential to discover the causes of its decline. The views of Connolly are quite noteworthy here when he says:

> The twenties carried on the period of wild experiment which had begun as an expanding experimental decade, had contracted to a smug superficiality as the fundamently reactionary nature of Post-Varsailles Europe became more apparent. What was original in the twenties easily degenerated into frivolity, dandyism, cynical cleverness, worship of the fashion.[40]

Connolly in the above passage clearly illustrates the reasons of the decline of the twenties owing to the reactionary nature of the 'Post-Versailles Europe' which led it to its degeneration into 'frivolity' and 'dandyism'. It must be noted here however, that it's too difficult to attest at this stage that the period degenerated into 'frivolity' or 'dandyism', but the thirties witnessed the emergence of some such writers who reacted tooth and nail to the frivolous spirit of the art of fiction-writing of the twenties. These writers in their technique and theme of fiction-writing appeared to be the spokesmen of their age so to say and even if they were not as original as their predecessors, they were the real representatives of their age. In one sense, they contributed a new dimension to it which the art of fiction was in dire need of, during that time. Connolly is in one way extolling the literary importance of the twenties on the one hand, and disparaging the achievements of the thirties on the other on a very flimsy ground that the writers of this period were not at all original craftsmen. Yet one may not endorse the allegation that writers like Evelyn Waugh, George Orwell, Graham Greene, C.P. Snow and many others deserve to be relegated to the background on such a negligible ground. Arnold Kettle has called such writers 'decadent', yet he holds a comparatively balanced view:

> That the work of, say Aldous Fluxley, George Orwell, Arthur Koestler, Graham Greene and Evelyn Waugh is in its total effect pessimistic, that the picture of the human situation that emerges from the novels of these writers is in the last degree unhopeful and, as a result, unhelpful, is not a matter of mere opinion but is as clearly demonstrable as any statement of literary criticism can well be.... They write about a society which manifests all the classic aspects of decadence; what is significant is that the writers themselves partake over-whelmingly in the values of the society they depict. They are not simply writers describing decadence, they are decadent writers.[41]

Kettle in his above observation points out a remarkable view that writers like Huxley, Orwell, Graham Greene and Evelyn Waugh in their writings represent the 'classic aspects of decadence' of the post-Versailles society. It is, therefore, not at all injudicious on the part of Kettle to pronounce them as writers of decadence. Compared to Kettle's, Connolly's picture is regrettably firm and unacceptable. Kettle thus assists readers and critics alike in assessing the mind and art of those writers who are often termed 'second rate' and 'minor' by many a critic.

John Wain also has spoken in defence of modern fiction: he pooh-poohs the irrational views of Connolly that the novel is dead. He holds his views that the fifties in England may not have been a decade studded with masterpieces but they have shown a great deal of activity not only in the field of novel-writing merely but in other branches of literature like drama, biography and criticism as well. He as such in the following passage leaves a note of cautions optimism in this way:

> Mr. Connolly wanders about the gardens of the West shouting 'All out!' and ringing his little bell, but no one seems to hear him. I am not saying that 'time' has proved him wrong or anything so highflying; only that the gardens of the west are still demonstrably open.[42]

John Wain has boldly refuted Connolly's irrational views that the gardens of the West have closed. He as such quotes Connolly's views and puts forward his own arguments. How Connolly in his famous critical book *The Unquiet Grave* does foretell the doomsday of fiction-writing becomes perfectly clear when he says:

> It's closing time in the gardens of the West and from now on an artist will be judged only by the resonance of his solitude, or the quality of his despair.... Flaubert, Henry James, Proust, Joyce and Virginia Woolf have finished off the novel. Now all will have to be re-invented as from the beginning.[43]

This reflects a mood of passimism and utter despair but it is against this disparaging drawing that John Wain comes up as a bold saviour:

> The ten years following that famous pronouncement saw the first appearance of a whole crowd of English writers: not all are going to be remembered, and one or two are fading already, but it would take a very determined pessimist to say that he detected no sign of life, no promise for the future, in the whole mass of work produced by—to dash down a few representative names William Golding, Iris Murdoch, Kingsley Amiss, John Osborne, Harold Pinter, Ted Houghes. And that is to confine onself to England, and to writers who had published nothing before 1950.[44]

He adds further again to substantiate his argument in the following way:

> In 1944 he gave it as his opinion that the novel was played out. Flaubert, Henny James, Proust, Joyce and Virginia Woolf have finished off the novel. Now all will have to be reinvented as from the beginning. But when the re-inventing was done, Mr. Connolly was not among those who cheered; and for an evident reason. The result was too conservative, not experimental enough. Just as he had predicted, a generation of writers appeared who did not try to continue the work of James, Proust, Joyce at all. (And with regard to Virginia Woolf they were openly sceptical, inclining to the view that particular tip had been a mistake.) But neither was it felt necessary to 're-invent' as 'from the beginning': Instead older models neglected for a century, were reverted to. A knock-about realist like Smollett became more of an 'influence' than Proust. Mr. Amis, the most widely admired new novelist of the fifties, wrote straightforward comedy of manners that would not have seemed unfamiliar to Fanny Burney.[45]

John Wain has discerned distinct signs of optinism in the growth of novel-writing owing to the revival of realism in the mode of writing. He attaches little importance to the forebodings and melancholy utterances of Connolly whose Cassandra-like tone leaves a disappointing note for the future of English novel. He rather feels elated at the emergence of these writers who instead of choosing Proust as their model of inspiration feel inclined to emulate the convention of Smollett and Fielding. He makes the tendency among these writers to revert to the age-old tradition of fiction-writing. It is just on account of this attitude of theirs that he prudently writes that the result of this was "too conservative, not experimental enough" and utters in almost the same vein "A knock-about realist like Smollett became more of an 'influence' than Proust." Wain thus pays his sincere complements to those writers who by reverting themselves to the age-old tradition of fiction-writing fulfil a great lacuna of the time. He traces the emergence of such writers in consonance with the spirit of the time. 'Realism' rather than 'experiment' becomes as a result of this attitude the main cry of the hour which it would be suicidal on the part of a conscientious critic to ignore. Wain thus states it clearly how the fashion of fiction-writing right from the thirties down to the present times seems to have undergone a wonderful change in the post-Versailles society of England in favour of delineating the bare facts of human existence rather than taking a wild flight in the world of airy nothing. The transcription of the matter of fact and the palpable world becomes the choiced subject matter of fiction as a result of the reaction to the writing of Mrs. Woolf, D.H. Lawrence and Joyce. As such, while discussing the post-war fiction one has not to overlook this important and noteworthy aspect of development in the growth and outlook of modern fiction in the least. In discussing the mind and art of Evelyn Waugh particularly, this noteworthy aspect of development in the mode of fiction-writing cannot be ignored. Waugh's first novel *Decline and Fall* written in the year 1928 was written against this very background of tremendous change in the technique of fiction-writing. Not merely that; it was written in a matter-of-fact style, contrary to the romantic spirit of writing being present in the unconscious and psycho-analytical works of Lawrence and Joyce. Often it is observed by some critics that the artists coming after Mrs. Woolf, Joyce and Lawrence abandoned the technical innovations of these pioneers of fiction on account of being incompetent, disqualified and inept in the handling of such delicate themes. This estimate, however, might seem to be a bit biased in nature. It does not seem that they were incompetent; in fact, they were intelligent and shrewd enough to catch the pulse of their time and act accordingly. James Gindin observes a very tolerant and reasonable view in this context in the following manner when he says:

> Most of these writers in an attempt to depict their engagement directly have avoided the kind of technical innovation favoured by an earlier generation of twentieth century writers. It is not that these writers dismiss James Joyce; it is simply that they do not (and perhaps could not) compete. Their interest in man's exterior relationships leads to a less associative internal style, to a style closer to the

> straightforward narrative of most of nineteenth century fiction. They often deliberately try to re-establish older and more conventional prose techniques.[46]

What James Gindin is aiming at in the above quotation is the interest of these writers in the delineation of exterior relationships of individuals rather than their interior life. The sense of appreciation takes a different bias from that of the twenties. He makes his point all the more clear when he adds further to the above passage in the following way:

> ...In addition to their formal conservative and their attempts to revive older novelistic traditions, their insistence on man's limitations, their comic perspective are all reminiscent of characteristics we tend to apply to eighteenth century writers. They appreciate and echo the scale, if not always the assurance, of Pope and two of them Amis and Wain; have spoken of their debt to the comic placement of rootless man in the fictional world of Henry Fielding.[47]

From the above observation it becomes crystal clear that the leanings towards the eighteenth century mode of writing seem to have acquired a considerable weight and significance in the minds of writers like John Wain, Evelyn Waugh, Amis and C.P. Snow in whose eyes the depiction of the world directly perceived by an artist is of much greater meaning and significance than the indirect perception of the supernatural and unconscious world. It's true that it would be odious indeed to disaparage one from the other in so far as the technique of writing is concerned, but the inevitable change in sensibility countenancing the direct perception of the bare facts of life all around, is by no means to be ignored by an intelligent critic. Evelyn Waugh accompanied by most of his counterparts in making a choice of the revival of conventional themes of the eighteenth century seems to be clever enough in catching the spirit of the time. A note of conservatism is then quite likely to be observed in him in spite of the employment of modern techniques of writing. The depiction of the modern man in his comic perspective which often reminds one of Henry Fielding, becomes consequently the chief preoccupation of Waugh's fiction. It is on account of this sincere and honest attempt on his part to emulate the style of novel-writing of Henry Fielding and Jane Austen, that one witnesses a remarkable tendency in him to revive the character, plot and other traditional forms of fiction-writing. It seems as if his views were similar to those of Pamela Johnson to a considerable length in making an appeal for the revival of a novel that tells a story—the novel in the tradition which began with Chaucer and continued through Fielding, Smollett and Dickens, culminating in Joyce Cary's novels.

Evelyn Waugh thus stands at the crossroads of the English novel who seems to have chosen his route very intelligently in favour of the traditional English novel. Even if he may be considered minor and second-rate on account of his having been a failure in choosing the technical innovations of Mrs. Woolf, Lawrence and Joyce, he is wise and prudent enough to have made a right selection of theme and style. In T.S. Eliot's words he too, while writing, is writing his time and in adopting the convention and themes of the classical writers he is true to the time of his age. David Lodge in his following observation touches on a very important point about the situation of the modern novelist when he writes:

> The situation of the novelist today may be compared to a man standing at a crossroads. The road on which he stands (I am thinking primarily of the English novelist) is the realistic novel, the compromise between fictional and empirical modes. In the fifties there was a strong feeling that this was the main road, the central tradition of English novel, coming down through the Victorians and Edwardians, temporarily diverted by modernist experimentatism but subsequently restored (by Orwell, Isherwood, Greene, Waugh, Powell, Angus Wilson, C.P. Snow, Amis, Sillitoe, Wain, etc; etc.) to its true course.[48]

Waugh thus holds a comfortable seat in the gallery of writers mentioned above owing much of the growth of his mind and art to the technique of conventional writing. Perhaps the tradition of fiction-writing, especially of the eighteenth century had a special significance in the eyes of Waugh and his other contemporaries. In fact, Evelyn Waugh in his comic indulgence is as much in the artistic kinship with Swift as in his allegorical interpretation of trivial themes with Chaucer and Fielding. The fundamental mode of fiction-writing in English has been realism from the very beginning which implies the primary concern of these writers with what people, objects and society are really like. Fielding does not favour any writer exceeding the limits of the probable and Waugh seems to be fully agreeing with him on this score. Waugh's theory of the art of fiction seems to be in keeping with the age-old tradition of novel-writing and he seldom takes any risk to present any unreliable and unconvincing picture of human life. He is, as it were, in link with the British tradition of novel writing which he never wants to lose sight of. In the following words, Mc Cormick highlights the special feature of British fiction which is found in the novels of Evelyn Waugh also:

> I take it as self-evident or as self-evident as anything ever is in literature that the fundamental mode of the English novel from its origins has been realism, just as the mode of the German novel has been philosophy, and of the French novel intellectualised morality. The English novelist has rarely been an intellectual in the French sense, rarely a philosopher in the German sense, but has been concerned with what people, objects, society are really like. Fielding mentions somewhere the necessity for the novelist never to exceed the limits of the probable and Smollett defined the novel as "a large diffused picture comprehending the characters of life, disposed in different groups and exhibited in various attitudes for the purposes of a uniform plan."[49]

Mr. Mc Cormick thus enumerates the special features of the English novel distinguishing it from those of the French and the German style of fiction-writing referring to the people, objects and society in general being the usual themes of their writing. Waugh, judged in this context, appears to be writing in matter-of-fact style reviving thus the real character of the British fiction in original. Mc Cormick illustrates further to give due weight to his statement when he substantiates his view in these words:

> The novel must have a central character for unity and form, without whom it will lack property, probability or success. To be useful, any discussion of tradition, I would think, must establish what 'reality' has meant to the English novelist and how, formally and technically rather than philosophically, his conception of the real world has appeared in the novel.[50]

Thus, Evelyn Waugh would appear to be in a direct link with the tradition of fiction-writing in English. In his choice of themes and techniques as such he is very much akin to his old masters of fiction, chiefly, Fielding, Smollett, Jane Austen, George Eliot. Above all, the concept of reality in his eyes is English in spite of his being under the impact of foreign writings. He maintains the character of the British fiction, it seems, with much reverence and dignity. The following opinion of his, I think, would sufficiently explain his stand as a novelist:

> It may happen in the next hundred years that the English novelists of the present day will come to be valued as we now value the artists and craftsmen of the late eighteenth century. The originators, the exuberant men are extinct and in their place subsists and modestly flourishes a generation notable for clegence and variety of contrivance. It may well happen that there are lean years ahead in which our posterity will look back hungrily to this period, when there was so much will and so much ability to please.[51]

NOTES

1. *A Little Learning*, The First Volume of an Autobiography. 1964—Evelyn Waugh, p. 33.
2. *Kangaroo*, D.H. Lawrence, Vol. 7—The Modern Age. Boris Ford 1969, p. 21.
3. E.M. Forster, Boris Ford. The Modern Age, *The Pelican Guide to English Life*. Vol. 7. 1961, p. 14.
4. *Ibid.*, p. 15.
5. *Tradition and Dream*, Walter Allen, Phoenix House, London, 1964, p. 1.
6. *Twentieth Century Literature*, A.C. Ward, Methuen and Co. Ltd., 1963, p. 2.

7. *Twentieth Century Literature*, A.C. Ward. 1901-1950 English Language Book Society of Methuen & Co. Ltd. 1963, p. 2.
8. *Ibid.*
9. A.C. Ward, *Twentieth Century Literature*, 1963, pp. 5-6.
10. R.A. Scott James. *Fifty Years of English Literature*, p. 2.
11. *Fifty Years of English Literature, 1900-1950*, R.A. Scott James 2nd Edition, 1956, p. 4.
12. *English Literature and Ideas in the Twentieth Century*, H.V. Routh, Methuen and Co. Ltd., London, 1950, p. 5.
13. *Roman Holiday: The Catholic Novel of Evelyn Waugh*. Vision Press Ltd., 1958, A.A. De Vitis, p. 7.
14. *Europe in the Nineteenth and Twentieth Centuries (1789-1950)* Grant and Temperley, Longman. Sixth edition. Nov. 1964, p. 504.
15. *New Hopes for a Changing World*. Allen and Unwin, 1960. Chapter—Current perplexities, p. 10.
16. *Ibid.*
17. *Civilization on Trial*—Arnold Toynbee. Chapter—Does History Repeat Itself, pp. 35-36.
18. A.J.J. Ratcliff, *Prologue to Prose of Our Time*, pp. 10-11.
19. *The Concise Cambridge History of English Literature*, George Sampson 3rd edition, 1972, p. 841.
20. The English novel. *A Short Critical History*, Walter Allen, Penguin Book, 1970, p. 258.
21. The English novel, Penguin Book, 1970. *The House of Fiction.* London, Rupert Hard Davis, 1957, p. 258.
22. *Ibid.*
23. 'The house of fiction', quoted from the Art of Fiction—1884. Edited. with an introduction by Leon Edel, Rupert Hard 1957, London, p. 25.
24. Walter Allen, Penguin Book, 1970. *The English Novel: A Short Critical History*, p. 294.
25. A Short Critical History of the novel, Walter Allen, Penguin Book, 1870, p. 262.
26. *A Concise Combridge History of English Literature*. George Sampson, New third Edition, revised by R.C. Churchill. Cambridge University Press, 1972, p. 836.
27. *Modern Fiction*, Virginia Woolf. The Common Reader, London, 1951, Hogarth Press, p. 189.

28. R.A. Scott James. *Fifty Years of English Literature*, Longmans, 1956, p. 125.
29. *Modern Fiction*, Quoted from the Common Reader, London. The Hogarth Press, 1951, pp. 194-95.
30. *Ibid.*, p. 187.
31. Notes on the decline of Naturalism-Philip Rahv, Realism and Remanticism in fiction. An approach to the novel. Engene Current-Garcia and Walton R. Patrick. Aubwon University, p. 186.
32. Notes on the decline of Naturalism-Philip Rahv. Realism and Romanticism in fiction. An approach to the novel. Eugene Current-Garcia Walton R. Patrick. Scott, Foresman and Com. 1962, pp. 186-87.
33. D.H. Lawrence. *Letter to Edward-Garnett* (5 June, 1914), Letters (1932).
34. Graham Hough, *The Total Dream*. The Muse and her Chair III, the Listner May 7, 1962, pp. 843-44.
35. *An Introduction to the Novel,* Vol. II, 1962, Arnold Kettle, Hutchinson University Library, London, pp. 113-14.
36. *The Present Age*, David Daiches. Cresset Press. London, 1958, p. 2.
37. The Vanishing Hero. Studies in novelists of the twenties. Sean O' Faolain. Eyre and Spilliswoods, London, 1956, pp. 19-20.
38. George Sampson. *The Concise Cambridge History of English Literature*, 3rd Edition, 1972, p. 867.
39. *Ibid.*
40. *The Making of George Orwell—An Essay in Literary History*. Keith Alldritt, pp. 75-76.
41. Arnold Kettle, *An Introduction to the Novel*, Hutchinson University Library, London, 1964. Vol. II, pp. 165-66.
42. *Essays on Literature and Ideas*, John Wain, London, Macmillan and Col. Ltd.; New York, St. Martin Press, 1963, pp. 161-63.
43. *The Unquiet Grave*, 1961, p. 21.
44. John Wain, *Essays on Literature and Ideas*, pp. 161-62.
45. Four Contemporary Critics, John Wain. *Essays on Literature and Ideas*. London. Macmillan & Co. Ltd.; New York, St. Martin Press, 1963, pp. 162-63.
46. James Gindin, *Post-War British Fiction—New Accents and Attitudes*. Cambridge University Press, 1962, p. 10.
47. *Ibid.*, p. 7.

48. *The Novelist at the Crossroads and Other Essays on Fiction and Criticism*, David Lodge. Routledge and Kegan Paul, London, 1971, p. 18.
49. Mc Cormick, *Catastrophe and Imagination—An Introduction of the Recent English and American Novel*. Longman, Green and Co., London, New York, Toronto, 1957, p. 136.
50. *Ibid*.
51. Evelyn Waugh, *The Ordeal of Gilbert Pinfold*, p. 9.

3

CHAPTER

Background of Critical Opinions on Waugh

"The end of criticism", writes T.S. Eliot in his famous critical book *Selected Essays*, "appears to be the elucidation of works of art and the correction of taste."[1] Observed in the light of this notable statement, it would appear that there are only a few critics who have chosen to adhere to this principle of criticism. Critical opinions on Waugh's mind and art are, it seems, too many to enable us to arrive at a final conclusion but most of them seem to be suffering from influences of personal whims and prejudices. Also, there appears to be a close identity of views even among critics with regard to their judgement about his mind and art which delightfully establishes the truth that Waugh is an endless topic of study for readers and critics alike. The following observation made by one Frederick J. Stopp should confirm this opinion:

> The novels are so subtle in technique and structure, and so rich in allusion, that there is no end to the fascinating task of exploring them. Several quite different books could be written on them: I have selected one possible approach. At the same time I do not think that the novels should be studied in isolation from Mr. Waugh's life and other works.[2]

On the basis of the above statement, one infers quite easily that Waugh's personality is so subtle and rich that he appears to be many things to many critics, as viewed by them from their respective angles. Some have dubbed him a satirist, a comedian, a philosopher, a catholic and some of the critics belonging to the Puritan block have called him a 'Conservative', 'snob', 'frivolous' and an 'entertainer' according as their judgement has allowed them to view him in their own way.

Evelyn Waugh, in the light of such remarks might appear to be a rather misunderstood genius of his time and for obtaining a fairly correct estimate of his mind and art it would be worthwhile to reconsider the points of view. To quote Prof. Carens first in this context whose opinion about Waugh seems to be very convincing:

> Puritans have found him frivolous, or at best, they have seen him as an "entertainer". But Evelyn Waugh has never been trivial, and he has always been much more than merely entertaining.[3]

A close scrutiny of the above opinion seems to submit a wonderful explanation of the fact that the charge of triviality often levelled by the Puritans against Waugh carries little sense. Not merely that; such opinions, if minutely observed, may seem to have been made under the influence of one's prejudices hardly helping one "in the common pursuit of true judgement."[4]

Now a reaction under the spell of puritanism need not surprise anyone. Besides, so very extremely varied are the opinions on Waugh that one would readily say with Frederick J. Stopp:

> Mr. Waugh holds and does not hesitate to express many opinions which provoke opposition. Irritation is a poor guide to insight.[5]

To my mind, Stopp's conclusion is an extreme example of understatement. Irritation is not merely a poor guide to insight—in fact it does not and mustn't guide insight, and very often it inhibits insight.

However, the reason behind the 'irritation' is undoubtedly the apparent simplicity and triviality of Waugh's personality that makes one observe him in a comic spirit only without recognising the inner depth. Waugh's personality, judged in this context, appears to be as trivial as that of Jane Austen who too in her writings gives an illusion of simplicity from the outside but is never so actually speaking from the inside. His early novels like *Decline and Fall*, *Vile Bodies*, and others along with the *Loved Ones*, and *Love Among the Ruins*, written during the final phase of his artistic career may be appearing entertaining, trivial and simple from the outside, but truly speaking, they bespeak of the gravity of purpose exhibited by Waugh in his works. The view appears to be similar to that of E.M. Forster's about the imperturbable character of the English which looked at outwardly, seems to be misleading and deceptive in nature but contains an immeasurable depth. To quote him as such for a full clarification of the mystery:

> We know what the sea looks like from a distance: it is of one colour and one level, and obviously cannot contain creatures as fish. But if we look into the sea over the edge of a boat we see dozen colours, and depth below depth and fish swimming in them. That sea is the English character apparently imperturbable and even.[6]

Evelyn Waugh too judged in the light of the above statement simply appears to be giving an illusion of simplicity and superficiality to his readers but truly speaking he is as grave and profound a writer as any one else in English fiction. Waugh's usual mode of writing is no doubt mock-heroic, but to say that he overlooks the intrinsic meaning of the values attaching meaning and sense to life, is fallacious indeed. A similar note is struck in the following remark made by Anthony Burgess:

> If Waugh is to be remembered as a comic novelist, that implies no relegation to a secondary status, as though it were a meaner achievement to make people laugh them to make them cry. He recognised his kinship with P.G. Wodehouse, but comedy with him was not merely entertainment, summer holiday stuff: it was a medium for the expression of ultimate truths, some of them very bitter. Apthorpe, like young Lord Tangent, has to die. The appalling "nonsense" which Cedric Line makes of the embarkation in *Put Out More Flags* is desperately funny, but it also encapsulates the real nonsense of the pre-Churchillian days, when England had still not learned what war was about.... Waugh's comic

underworld—smugglers, deserters, burglars, night-club courtesans are accorded the dignity of language appropriate to personages who have in their various bizarre ways, arrived at acceptable modes of order. The humour is, in the best sense, aristocratic.[7]

What Anthony Burgess seeks to point out here is Waugh's search for the ultimate truths of life in his novles rather than a mere superficial longing in him to entertain and please his readers. As a matter of fact, the chief aim of Waugh's fiction is to present his theme in a most humorous fashion so as not to create any boring, dull and insipid mood in his readers; but unfortunately his critics misinterpret and misunderstand what he actually intends to bring home to them through his fiction. His sugar-coated humour seems to be keeping his real self in disguise but this must not make us forget the real aim of his novel being a search for the 'ultimate truths'. The fact is that the theory of naturalism makes him present the insane world of today in a comic vein as if he were merely a joker, a buffoon having little sense of the outside world being frivolous and irremediably futile in nature, but truly speaking, his buffoonery is a camouflage intentionally used by him to treat his subject matter as it is rather than as it should be. His style of writing as such appears to be immeasurably deceptive in form as well as content. Naturally and aptly, Patricia Corr makes the following reflection in a forthright manner:

> Much of the early criticism of Mr. Waugh's novels tended to concentrate on particular and often superficial aspects of his writing. He was justly lauded as a brilliant satirist, the laureate of the Gay Twenties, and condemned as a cruel joker or a snob whose myopic view of society was confined to the Mayfair set known as the Bright Young People.... Mr. Waugh is both a sound moralist and an observant humorist and it is his humour which makes palatable the unpleasant medicines he prescribes for his readers.[8]

In the above passage, Patricia Corr clearly reveals the great truth about Waugh that he treats his world fantastically, sarcastically and too often in a spirit of levity and buffoonery but his ultimate aim never being that in true sense of the term. What after all attracts one in his fiction is the ironic presentation of the world he depicts, although a perceptive insight only could be able to achieve this end. Patricia Corr goes on to remark as to how Waugh's "Characters move in a vicious circle of aimlessness, boredom and futility as they fall a prey to the vicious circle unwittingly they are moving in." Here let us quote another critic—A.A. De Vitis who writes in his famous critical book *The Roman Holiday*:

> It becomes the concern of the reader to understand the novelist's intention to know with what object he portrays the aspects of evil.
>
> The essential question is from what attitude he depicts and whether his art and mind are pure enough and strong enough to depict it without connivance. The more deeply the modern novelist probes human misery, the more does it require super-human virtues in the novelist.[9]

A.A. De Vitis, with the help of Maritain's contention given in his Art and Scholasticism seeks to clarify the attitude a reader must try to pick up if he is inclined to understand and elucidate the theme of a work of art written from some particular point of view. Paul Pennyfeather's innocence for instance is nothing but an artistic device in Evelyn Waugh to present an ironic spectacle of the irremediable futility of the outside world, full of tricks and moral turpitude inviting an innocent man to get entangled in its net. It is the attitude of irony one has to get at with a view to understanding the form and content of the fiction he writes. Guy's placing against a horde of dishonest, hypocrite soldiers simply proves the sham world of military life completely wanting in the virtues a soldier must have. It is on this very ground that very often Waugh is accused of ruthlessness towards his characters. To quote Christopher Hollis in this context:

> Waugh's characterisation was often criticised on grounds that show, I think, a misunderstanding of his intentions. He was sometimes criticised for his lack of pity, but the criticism, I think, a little misses the point.... There is obvious sincerity in incidental remarks, such as that put into the

> mouth of Adam Symes, in Vile Bodies, that such futility must inevitably be leading to catastrophe, and there is an artistic wit in the conclusion of Vile Bodies which tells us of the quite secondary question between whom the war is fought.[10]

An analysis of this remark should show that Waugh is not at all cruel towards Agatha Runcible who instead of hearing sympathetic words from her friends at the time of her death, hears taunting replies only quite unbecoming the character of her friends. Here it is not the lack of pity however but the determination to portray what is actually happening in our civilization that is striking. There is no doubt about this that we live in a most cruel and pitiless world as there is no milk of human kindness flowing in the human heart and if Waugh, with a view to maintaining the verisimilitude of his fiction creates such characters as are mocking at Agatha Runcible when she is at the point of death, this presentation does not give any smack of a lack of pity or cruelty in the art of characterization on the part of Waugh. Besides, the question between whom the war is fought, is also as absurd as anything in this world of futility and utter purposelessness. The criticism of the lack of pity as such seems untenable on these grounds. The presentation of a pitiless world reminds one of Waugh's own sad utterances, "To have been born into a world of beauty and to die amid ugliness is the fate of all us exiles."[11] Equally pertinent is this remark from A.A. De Vitis:

> He aimed his acid wit at his characters making them make themselves ridiculous. The moral commentary was oblique, and the religious convictions that were to inform Brideshead Revisited were not at all portrayed in either character of action.... The world of human experience is held at such a distance as to preclude the possibility of its being taken seriously at a distance at which persons become puppets and thereby appropriate objects of diversion.[12]

It is easily inferred from the above passage that Waugh maintains distance or detachment so to say while presenting his picture ironically. Waugh seldon takes, it seems, the risk of involving himself personally and maintains objectivity in the protrayal of his theme. Frederick Stopp also has not missed to mark the artistic value of his silence which "is paralled by his avoidance of comment, as narrator, on the processes in the mind of his creatures."[13]

The quality of detachment is as such a striking quality in Evelyn Waugh without appreciating which it may not be very profitable to study his mind and art. Sean O' Faolain too has dubbed Waugh's cruelty "more often a deliberate and well-pointed and wholly admirable part of his technique" and stressed his double-edged achievement for sound reasons. Another point that is very often discussed about Waugh is whether he writes comedy or satire. Now admittedly this is the most crucial part of the controversy about the mind and art of Evelyn Waugh. The fact is that Waugh himself objects to the description of his work as social satire or comedy. He leaves this question to be answered by his readers themselves. Graham Martin explains this issue quite convincingly:

> Waugh has objected to the common description of his early work as social satire on the ground that this is impossible in a society which provides the satirist with no acceptable norms of behaviour, attitude and belief.[14]

What Martin aims at in the above passage is the instability of moral values in a fast changing society of today that totally precludes the possibility of having any fixed standard and criterion of values. The fact is that Waugh himself on this very ground objects to the description of his work as social satire or comedy. He himself writes about his function as an artist in the following way:

> My problem has been to distill comedy and sometimes tragedy from the knockabout farce of people's outward behaviour.[15]

The above-mentioned passage appears to be a sufficient proof of the fact that he does not write with any fixed aim of either a comedian or a satirist. It would therefore be risky on our part to attach a particular kind of label to his fiction either of social satire or comedy. His aim as it is inferred from the above passage, is to deal with the outward actions and behaviour of men and women resulting in comedy or satire according as the treatment they get at the hands of Evelyn Waugh. It is as such too difficult indeed to describe his work either as social satire or comedy. The underlying implication is that there is no possibility of writing satire in such a period of instability in almost all spheres of life—social, political, moral and intellectual. Martin's views may be quoted once again for a full clarification of this issue in this context:

> The satirical bias, which we begin by assuming is simply hidden from view by the parodic report, turns out to have no definable status. When Waugh appears to offer one, it is only a trick. He lures the reader into a judgement—in the context of neutral narration we are eager to accept one—and then leaves him there, the target of a hostility more supple and more deepseated than he had guessed. In both a local and general view, this is more important than the dissection of Mayfair high life.... To angle the view (as, for example Angus Wilson does) would be to expose a particular animus, and so a criterion of judgement. But there is no criterion. And, as a consequence, the neutral manner is not simply a satirist's tactic, but the statement of what we have to call for lack of another term, an attitude.[16]

In the long passage noted above, Martin simply warns us against making any sort of commitment with regard to the labelling of his novel with some specific name: Comedy, tragedy, tragicomedy, satire or anything else. According to Martin, Waugh simply 'lures the reader into a judgement' which implies the lack of any specification in so far as the labelling of his fiction is concerned. There is only an attitude he seems to be stating but it is too difficult to name it. Notwithstanding all this, it may be argued that (whatever the attitude of Waugh as a writer be) he seems to be making fun of everything he sees, hears, and finds all around him. He is a naturalist, photographing a natural picture of the sophisticated gallery of human society whose actions and manners provoke him into an outburst of laughter and fun whether the laughter might he containing the hue of his elegent and refined humour or pain. Waugh's reticence keeps him silent without allowing him to expose his self. He seems to be puzzling his readers much as to his attitude he is actually writing from. One would readily agree with James Hall who has found a note of tragicomedy in Waugh's fiction. To quote Hall:

> He may be merely an entertainer with a style, but comedy is usually serious, however much some analysis may burlesque its kind of seriousness: Waugh's early novels have evocative power.[17]

To my mind it appears that Waugh's fiction is a fine blending of comedy and tragedy—a fact which will be borne out by the change of his style and technique in accordance with the corresponding change in his attitude to life from time to time. The Evelyn Waugh of the final stage is therefore never the same as that of the early phase making fun of the Mayfair set known as the Bright Young People in a spirit of levity and buffoonery. Waugh's fiction appears to have been written completely in tune with the light, trivial and fantastic spirit of time claiming thus to be easily put in the line of the celebrated practitioners of fiction namely Henry Fielding. Jane Austen and Charles Dickens. Whatever the attitude of Waugh as a novelist be, the present chapter may be summed up in these words: Waugh is a novelist of the post-world war society writing in a mock-heroic style with a view to attaining fidelity and verisimilitude in his writing.

NOTES

1. *Selected Essays* quoted from the Function of criticism. London. Faber and Faber Ltd. 24 Russell Square, 1951, p. 24.
2. Preface. *Evelyn Waugh—Portrait of an Artist.* Frederic J. Stopp, p. 7.
3. Prof. Carens, *Satiric Art of Evelyn Waugh*, p. 3.
4. T.S. Eliot, *The Function of Criticism*, p. 25.
5. Preface. *Evelyn Waugh—Portrait of an Artist*, Frederick, J. Stopp. London. Chapman and Hall Ltd., 1958, p. 7.
6. Abinger Harvest, *E.M. Forster*, A Penguin book, 1936, p. 18.
7. The spectator, April 15, 1966, Evelyn Waugh, 1903-1966. "The comedy of ultimate truth's", Anthony Burgess, p. 462.
8. Patricia Corr. *Evelyn Waugh: Sanity and Catholicism Autumn*, 1962, p. 388.

9. *The Roman Holiday*, A.A. De Vitis (Maritain, 171, Art and Scholasticism), p. 15.
10. Evelyn Waugh, Christopher Hollis, p. 5.
11. *A Little Learning*, the first Volume of an autobiography, 1964. Evelyn Waugh, p. 33.
12. D.S. Savage, "The Innocence of Evelyn Waugh", *The Roman Holiday*, p. 22.
13. Frederick, J. Stopp, p. 181.
14. Evelyn Waugh.
15. *The Modern Age*. Vol. 7, Pelican Guide to English Lit., Boris Ford, p. 398.
16. *The Modern Age*. Vol. 7, Pelican Guide to English Lit., Novelists of three decades: E. Waugh, Graham Greene, C.P. Snow—Graham Martin. Bors. Ford, p. 398.
17. *The Tragic Comedians*, James Hall, p. 45.

4 CHAPTER

Waugh the Man—A Close Scrutiny

In his foreword to the famous biography of Laurence Sterne, Margaret R.B. Shaw makes the following observation which, to my mind is applicable to Evelyn Waugh as well while judging him as a man.

"I frankly discharge", Margaret R.B. Shaw writes, "a man from my humours (says Montaigne) and consider him according to his particular model." A difficult undertaking, certainly—our special environment and education, our individual characters, our personal tastes, opinions and idiosyncrasies, so mould the minds of each one of us to a settled pattern that it is the most ticklish and delicate business in a world to rid ourselves of pre-conceived notions and come within even reasonable distance of understanding another man's mind. Yet, however hard it be to follow, a biographer who wishes to do justice to a man of genius must try to keep this principle in view in all examination of his life and works.[1]

In the paragraph quoted above, one comes across the complications which usually arise in the minds of readers and critics alike in view of their individual characters and personal tastes, opinions and indiosyncrasies, while judging the mind of a writer.

The study of Waugh as a man becomes essential with a view to judging his mind and art in a clear perspective without giving rein to our feelings and attitudes. Naturally, biographical data in view of this analysis would assume a special significance in this context. It becomes desirable then to keep in mind the following points of view of David Daiches which deal with the considerable importance of psychology in course of the critical evaluation of a writer's work of art:

> In explaining the nature of a work of literary art, the critic is often led into psychology, into a discussion of the state of mind out of which literary creation arises.... The notion that the artist is neurotic, sick, maladjusted, that art is somehow a by-product of this sickness and maladjustment, has become immensely popular during the last hundred and fifty years, and modern psychology seems to have justified it.[2]

The above quotation illustrates the point quite clearly as to how the exploration of one's mind in its real prespective, as far as it is possible, becomes difficult without a careful study of the biographical data. The study of Waugh's mind and art then becomes imperfect without a careful scrutiny of him as a man. The bio-critical method in this context appears to be the only key to the secrets of Waugh's mind helping one peep into the very substratum of his personality. Frederick Stopp's portrait of Waugh is worth quoting from the following extract:

> Evelyn Arthur St. John Waugh "was born on 28 October, 1903, the feast of S.S. Simon and Jude, the second son of Arthur Waugh publisher, editor, and man of letters. On his father's side he descended from a family which had been farmer proprietors for centuries in the village of East Gordon in Berwickshire, until, at the end of the eighteenth century. Alexander Waugh a Minister, came south and established himself in London. His son, the Rev. James Hay Waugh then moved to the West Country to become Rector of Corsley, near Frome.... Arthur Waugh was a fairly good poet, with many critical interests, the author of an excellent book on Tennyson and of editions of others of the English masters. After twelve years spent in gaining literary experience in the capital he became, in 1902 at the age of thirty-five chairman and managing director of the old established publishing firm of Chapman and Hall, then in the doldrums and relying too

heavily on the profitable but diminishing asset of the Dickens Copyright. He directed the firm with his combination of literary sympathy and business aptitude until his retirement in 1929."[3]

Here, we get a fairly correct estimate of the mind of Evelyn Waugh as an artist when we come to know about his belonging to a family of farmer proprietors and his being the son of "a fairly good poet with many critical interests." The passage thus gives a sufficient hint about his upbringing in a literary environment conducive to the growth of his artistic mind. Not merely that, it gives sufficient data of his heredity which provided him with the resources having their direct bearings on his creative mind. The proverb 'the child is father of the man' in this context is aptly applicable as the seeds of literary gift seem to have been present in his mind from the very early beginnings. Psychologically speaking then he seems to have inherited his artistic traits. On these grounds, the impact of heredity and environment both on the development of his mind and art is found in the clearest possible manner which provides a satisfactory bio-critical data to a critic in course of his judgement of Waugh as a man. Evelyn Waugh, on the basis of the above observation may undoubtedly be called the natural corollary of his environment which induced him to be an artist of a high calibre. Here are some other details too which throw a vivid light on his development as an artist. In this context, the influence of the Lancing school instead of the Sherborne in the making of his career as a comic artist is also of no small significance. While taking a record of the days of his schooling, one gets an impression as to how the choice of Lancing, a public school made him a man of debatable temperament giving him thus a full chance to keep his mind free as contrasted against the restricted atmosphere of the Sherborne. It's true that in making the choice of Lancing the religious bent of his mind also was kept in view but the free atmosphere of Lancing allowed him to grow to the level of full maturity in his mind and art. Also the publication of *The Loom of Youth* of Alec Waugh was also a forceful factor behind the choice of Lancing instead of the Shereborne. The following remark of Frederic Stopp is worth quoting here:

> When the time came for Evelyn to enter a public school, family tradition would have indicated Sherborne, had not Alec Waugh's precocious novels of public school life, *The Loom of Youth*, published in 1917, caused a considerable stir, and made the choice of some other school advisable for the younger son. Lancing was chosen and later appeared in the work as 'a school of ecclesiastical temper on the South Downs. Indeed, its strong religious life was one of the factors which led to its choice, since, as the father noted, the young Evelyn had always shown a deeply religious temperament.[4]

In this passage, we get an insight into the religious bent of his mind and at the same time his critical and ratiocinative brain that seldom allowed him to accept anything on its face value. The evidence of his debatable temperament is found in this sense also that during his school days he would very often discuss the current points of view of society with a reasonable logic and argument and try to convince the mind of his listeners. In spite of being a Roman Catholic, Stopp records his iconoclastic attacks on the established reputations of society in the following way:

> We hear of iconoclastic attacks on established reputations, especially of those enshrined within the covers of the Oxford Books of English and of Victorian verse; of duels with authority, carried out with the same impassive exterior, the same innocence of the intent to be amusing as later characterised his books. An entry in a diary of 1921 predicts that he will be the Max Beerbohm of his generation, if not something greater, records a parody of an epigram by Landor and ends, significantly, "J.F. likes it a lot."[5]

The purpose behind this passage is a minute study of Waugh's critical bent of mind which, if properly analysed, seeks to search for meaning and purpose in every phenomenon of life whether it be religion or science or any trivial aspect of human life. A careful study of his mind thus makes one aware of his inquiring mind restlessly probing the mystery of social, political, moral and intellectual questions of human life. There are a few instances which clearly prove his instinctive urge for religion but he is not a man attaching a blind faith and reverence to it.

Alec Waugh in his famous book *My Brother Evelyn and Other Profiles* gives many such examples in the form of anecdotes that leave little scope of doubt in the mind of his readers about his brain being argumentative and ratiocinative in nature. These anecolotes bear a clear-cut testimony to his utter disregard of any kind of formality or ritual being followed in a customary spirit rather than in a spirit of true reverence and devotion to it. The following observation made by Alec would bear a clear-cut testimony to his intolerance of such pursuits of human life as are actuated by the ritual spirit rather than a feeling of true and sincere devotion to it. It appears really strange how he became audacious enough to point out the besetting sin of his mother on the occasion of the Lent. Alec records his impressions thus:

> When he was quite young—I do not know the exact date—his mother said to him before the beginning of Lent. We are now starting lent. We should also be on our guard against our besetting sin—you know, don't know, what is your besetting sin? He shook his head; no, he had no knowledge of it. His mother explained, it was his quick and unkind tongue. He accepted her criticism: pondered it for a moment and then said, "You know, mother, what is your besetting sin?"
>
> This was a shock to her. Conscious though she was of her shortcomings in the world at large, she thought that in his nursery and in the eyes of the second son, she was the image of perfection. But she supposed that she must face the mirror. "No, Evelyn." She said, "what is it?" The answer came back straight. A lack of faith in Catholic Doctrine. And of course, she would say afterwards in recounting the incident, he was completely right, I do lack faith.[6]

The passage is interesting and thought-provoking both in so far as the reaction of Evelyn Waugh to the question of the besetting sin asked by his mother is concerned, but above all, it gives a penetrating insight into his utter dislike and hatred of the outward show and behaviour of mankind. The study of the passage thus hints at his comic attitude of the follies and foibles of his society the evidence of which we find in his taking a light enjoyment in the trifling pursuits of the Bright Young People of his society. It is on account of this comic attitude of life that he draws a very amusing portrait of Father Rothschild in his second novel *Vile Bodies* whose unseemly behaviour becomes an object of ridicule in his eyes. Besides, this remark reveals a sure indication of his being an ironist blessed with a two-pronged vision from the very beginning of his childhood days. Waugh on the basis of the above observation appears to be very much sensitive from the days of his very infancy on account of which he becomes restless to find out the sense, meaning, and purpose in every sphere of life. In his visit once to the Abyssinia monastry of Debra Lebanos he had had the chance to see the dereliction of duties on the part of priests which he has recorded thus:

> At Debra Lebanos I suddenly saw the classic basillica and open altar as a great positive attachment, a triumph of light over darkness consciously accomplished, and I saw theology as the science of simplification by which nebulous and elusive ideas are formalised and made intelligible and exact. I saw the church of the first century as a dark and hidden thing; as dark and hidden as the seed germinating in the womb; legionaries off duty slipping furtively out of barracks, greeting each other by signs and passwords in a locked upper room in the side street of some Mediterranean seaport; slaves at dawn creeping from the grey twilight into the candle-lit smoky chapels of the catacombs. The priests hid their office, practising trades, their identity was known to initiates; they were criminals against the law of their country.[7]

Waugh in the above passage appears to be a disillusioned man who is as it were revising his impressions about the holy priests who are found by him going off their moral track. The impressions formed here are undoubtedly of a traveller but there is a conscious man behind the formation of such reactions. In his counter-reply to his mother that her 'besetting sin' was the lack of her faith, one could easily mark the presence of a man who seems to be boldly reacting to the preachings and sermons of an ideologist who himself or herself deserves to be preached. Apart from this, there is a further indication too as to how religion becomes a dominant source of moral inspiration to him almost equivalent to science in nature and gives a formal shape to the 'nebulous and elusive ideas' of mankind making them 'intelligible and exact.' A further probe should explain his sincere devotion to the moral doctrines which give order and harmony to human life. One could thus easily trace the origins of his satirical attitude to the oddities and idiosyncrasies of human life being the raw materials of his fiction. There is no doubt then about his mind being pious and fearless which enables one a great deal in exploring the causes of the creation of his works of art. Incidentally in one of his debates during his school days as to what religion is, he made a fine and thought-provoking reservation, "Religion was the focus for all that was finest and best in man". The observation made in such a candid and forthright manner gives a correct evidence of his mind being ratiocinative and critical both at the same time.

His school days apart, in his Oxford days too, his mind seems to have reacted considerably to the decaying culture of the time. His college days made him aware of the dandyism of the youth which he seems to have dealt with in the first half of his famous novel *Brideshead Revisited*, giving a detailed account of the sacred and profane memories of charles Ryder. How much abnormally sensitive Evelyn Waugh was is reflected in the following record made by Harold Acton quoted by Frederick J. Stopp:

> Neither Peter, nor Robert, nor Evelyn were butterflies and all three were characteristic members of my own generation. The butterfly never settles on any flower for long. Robert, Peter and Evelyn settled on any subject that aroused them like grim death and clung tenaciously until they had extracted every drop of essence. Robert Clung to Byzantium; Peter to Baudelaire's dandyism; Evelyn to Rossetti and social satire, and eventually to Rome.[8]

Here we can trace the abnormally sensitive mind of Evelyn Waugh which does not react like the normal and dull mind of an ordinary man but with a whimper at the sight of any declining trend. He appears to be a man in whose eyes the decay of the classical culture is a sad phenomenon in the wake of the abnormal growth of modern science and technology. This makes him feel discontented with the bric-a-brac of modern civilization and provokes him to satirise the hollowness and emptiness of modern man. The germs of satire thus appear to be present in him from the very beginning of his childhood days. It is his experience of the contradiction, the abnormality and the laughable behaviour of the people he happens to come across in course of his tour to different parts of Europe, that makes him attack the established reputation of social, political, and moral institutions of mankind. The works of art like *The Black Mischief*, *A Handful of Dust* and *The Loved One* are the result of such experiences as draw the portrait of a man having come in direct touch with the cross-fertilization of different cultures. Evelyn Waugh on the basis of this observation seems to be an extraordinary brain that takes an active interest in the exploration of the causes of decline in the case of modern culture. This attitude to the life of a modern man gives a further confirmation of his religious temperament that seldom allows him to deviate from the moral bindings of religion. This is why his attachment to Roman Catholicism becomes a very important factor to rely upon in the analysis of his mind and art. The creation of *A Handful of Dust* bears to a considerable extent the evidences of his break in marriage and as such it presents sufficient data of biographical details about his utter dislike of modern humanism. Not merely that, he has gone on to record how after his break in marriage he went out on a tour to different parts of Europe including Brazil to relax his mind bearing the strains and stresses of his marital frustration. The portrait of Tony Last having left his home in quest of a city to get the peace of mind because of his nuptial discord at the hands of Brenda Last seems to be a sure revelation of the mystery of the creation of *A Handful of Dust* Mr. Waugh himself is reported to have said many years later about this book which suggests to a considerable extent the cause of its having been written in the form of fiction:

> I had written a short story about a man trapped in the jungle, ending his days reading Dickens aloud. The idea came quite naturally from the experience of visiting a lonely

> settler of that kind and reflecting how easily he could hold me a prisoner. Then, after the short story was written and published, the idea kept working in my mind. I wanted to discover how the prisoner got there, and eventually the thing grew into a study of other sorts of savages at home and the civilized man's helpless plight among them.... A handful of Dust dealt entirely with behaviour. It was humanist and contained all I had to say about humanism.[9]

Evelyn Waugh's own explanation as to the creation of *A Handful of Dust* in the passage above clearly illustrates his acute feeling of distintegration all around. He seems to have witnessed the signs of disintegration with an acute sensation which owes its origin to a considerable extent to his own broken self due to the failure in his conjugal life and the impact of the loss of culture and morality in the general life of humanity outside in public life. The writing of his novels of disintegration thus bears a clear-cut proof of his unconscious mind bearing the weight of wounded feelings and experiences of his private life. Alec Waugh in his famous book *My Brother Evelyn and Other Profiles* already referred to in the preceeding pages, gives oblique references to the nuptial discord which forced him to take a refuge into the Roman Catholicism. To quote Alec Waugh in this context for a full confirmation of the impact the betrayal on the part of Mrs. Evelyn in his case did leave upon his mind:

> It was a blow that left a permanent scar on Evelyn. He had given himself to She-Evelyn and to his marriage without reservations. He had trusted her completely; he was vulnerable from every angle. He had no armour against her betrayal of his trust. He was too much an artist to indulge a personal resentment in his novels, yet the characters of Tony Last and Charles Ryder show how incessantly the old wound throbbed. His tongue would never have been so sharp, his reposts so acid had not that throbbing needed to be assuaged.
>
> "The whole thing was tragic", he writes further, "Yet even so, it is impossible to doubt that the divinity that shapes our ends' was serving its own purposes in bringing Evelyn

Gardiner into Evelyn's life. But for her he might not have begun to write.... Maugham would not have been the writer he became had his marriage been a success. Nor would Evelyn."[10]

A close scrutiny of the passage quoted above provides a vivid insight into the working of Evelyn's mind, illustrating clearly how art and neuroses both work together in the creation of a literary work of art. These minute details might often appear unmeaningful to a common reader but they reflect to a considerable extent the character of Evelyn Waugh as a man which assists a critic a good deal in exploring the innermost recesses of Waugh's mind. True it is that these elements often identified as biographical in nature lose their meaning when re-arranged and transformed in a work "but it will be said", write Rene Welleck and Austin Warren, "such instances of pretentious folly do not dispose of the problem of personality in literature. We read Dante or Goethe or Tolstoy and know that there is a person behind the work. There is an indubitable physiognomical similarity between the writings of one author...still there are connecting links, parallellisms, oblique resemblances, topsyturvy mirrors. The poet's work may be a mask, a dramatised conventionalisation, but it is frequently a conventionalisation of his own experiences, his own life."[11]

Waugh thus appears as a neurotic for whom fiction becomes the forte of his creative imagination. He seems to be peeping through the open window of his personal reminiscences whether they be sweet or bitter. The inference coming out from these passages is this as if a disjointed consciousness either due to the untoward happenings of his private life or due to the disintegrated spirit of the post-war world were at work in his fiction without considering which it is undoubtedly difficult to understand his mind and art correctly. Alec's observation as to his break in his conjugal life as a result of Mrs. Evelyn's betrayal thus assumes a special significance in view of the exploration of Waugh's mind provoking him to give a new mould and twist to his art. Besides, it provides a very satisfactory and convincing clue to the secret of all secrets why he took a last refuge in Roman Catholicism. Alec Waugh in his biographical passage touches upon some such impressions and details that he enables one to form a correct and sound analysis of his personality. He has drawn the portrait of Evelyn as a child quite different in his nature and attitude to life from that of his own. By perusing the passage critically one draws the impression of priest-like nature in Evelyn. It seems as if he were a man who spent the major part of his time in making a voyage within rather than without. His priest-like nature thus makes him appear as an unwordly figure and very often a nuisance to Alec his own brother as well as the outside world. He writes in his profiles of Evelyn that he was a devout child from the very beginning of his life and he would often go to matins even. The portrait runs as follows:

> As a child he went to matins, in a small village type church-room, where the service was conducted by a man not in holy orders, but from the age of, I should say seven, he attended with the rest of us, choral celebration at St. Jude's, in the Garden suburb, which was near Anglo-catholic; its priest being Basil Bouchier, a cousin of the actor, who was satirised as the Rev. Boon Bagshaw in A.S.M.... He had a shrine in his bedroom at which he lit incense.[12]

The above portrait guides a sensitive critic to a considerable extent to read the inner workings of Evelyn Waugh's mind which became religious from the very beginning of childhood days. Temperamentally then Waugh appears to be an introvert in contrary to the temperment of Alec Waugh being extrovert in nature. It is quite natural then on the part of Alec to feel irritated by him. The following remark provides a direct probe into this aspect of his personality which often seemed to be a nuisance to him. To quote him thus again for a further revelation of this mysterious side of his nature:

> He was, inevitably, something of a nuisance to me. Presumably I was to him. In our first home, in West Hampstead, my nursery cricket—a game I played by myself—was restricted by the danger of hitting a ball into his cot. When we moved to Underhill, a larger house, I at first left the nursery to him, and spent the winter day time reading in my father's book room. But after a while I became interested in billiards, and

a small table was installed in the nursery. Evelyn must have regarded this as an invasion of his territorial rights.[13]

Evelyn Waugh, judged in view of these minute details mentioned above, appears to be abnormal who forms the category of a snob in his own case ready to impose his own points of view on others. He as such presents himself before us as a singular figure in the plurality of the masses due to the formation of a private universe in himself. It is owing to his lack of adjustment and harmony with the other members of his family that he becomes a typical figure in himself. I don't think it is because of the formation of a private universe within himself that his impressions, attitudes and reactions to the outside world of men and women are, as the indications come out, that of a snob. The formation of this inner world owing to such factors often becomes incomprehensible to a layman. Even Alec himself admits his failure in providing a clue to the secrets of his self when he mentions his following points of view quite candidly:

> I wrote in my early years in explanation of the fact that it contained so little about my brother I lack the key to Evelyn. I cannot enter imaginatively into the mind of a person for whom religion is the dominant force in his life, for whom religion is a crusade.... He (Evelyn) was inevitably, something of a nuisance to me. Presumably I was to him.[14]

These biographical sketches contain the germs of truth about the development of Evelyn Waugh as an artist. The element of snobbery, found in his character, explains the varied sides of his personality which may be termed as his abnormality, sensitivity, and his aristocracy. In his war trilogy for example one gets a clear-cut evidence of his snobbery which seems to be present in the portrayal of Guy Crouchback, the hero representing his reactions to the follies and foibles of military life. John St. John who is reported to have participated in the war with Evelyn Waugh records his own impressions about his character in military life. He writes clearly and convincingly as to how he had felt dissatisfied and discontented with the officers and men in the military life who in his opinion were not at all fit to hold their so-called position even due to many disqualifications being inherent in them. He did not tolerate the presence of the misfits who posed as his officers but inherited no social status and a high family background. Waugh as a man never seems to be free from this aristocratic mentality which does not want to tolerate the presence of such officers and men as appeared to be upstarts in their sudden rise to the position of extraordinary height. In the following passage, one comes across this side of his personality when during his military life he was persuaded by his commander to ask him any question about the military life he felt like asking. At hearing this Waugh immediately stood up and said derisively which is recorded by John St. John in these words:

"Any question?" It was a solemn moment and the inquiry was itself clearly rhetorical, but Evelyn was undaunted. "Would you not agree Sir, that it would be ever so much nicer if there were no Marine Soldiers and if everyone could be an officer? Our co was a very tolerant man with a sense of humour but this kind of provocation was difficult to take. Evelyn could seldom resist the temptation to poke fun; for example. I once heard him innocently inquire, to the perplexity of a pompous visiting brass hat, if it were true that 'in the Rumanian army no one beneath the rank of major was permitted to use lipstic.' His man found him equally puzzling. A petty offence could make him apoplectic. I once heard him addressing a parade on the question of swearing: "The continued use of obscenities in conversation is tedious and undignified. These words punctuate your speech like a hiccup. Instead they should be savoured and reserved for the creative act itself or for moments of the most extreme frustration. As they listened dutifully to the petulant, elegant voice the ranks of motionless faces under their Khaki fore-and-aft caps were bewildered."[15]

In these words, one meets a figure who seems to be loathing the sight of the hypocrites and the upstarts whose behaviour is shallow and hollow both because of having no family background and any social status. This passage in one way is a sure indication of his snobbery which John St. John illustrates more clearly by adding further to it when he comments:

> Evelyn certainly lived up to his reputation for snobbery, though it struck me as being in part ironical, if not a pose. In the mess as well as on the parade ground he treated inferiors in rank or superiors without the right social background with a scorn that while amusing was uncharitable, but this also made him impervious to too much military bullshit. Personally I revelled in his companionship and found him a delightful fellow sufferer especially when we were messed about unnecessarily or when conditions were physically unpleasant.[16]

In the passage quoted above, we get a complete picture of Waugh as a man whose works of art clearly illustrate the varied aspects of his personality. The passage seems to be clearly narrating the untold story of Waugh's reactions to the then military life as a man getting their reflection in the world of his fiction. These details certainly present his snobbery confirming his class-consciousness bordering upon aristocracy. This element of snobbery in him makes him, as it appears, unusually sensitive to the decadent spirit of the art and culture of his time.

Evelyn Waugh, judged on the basis of the above observations, seems to be a sentimental figure suffering from a melancholic strain. He writes humorously but it is seldom free from the sad tone of his poignant humour. His pensive mood appears to be all the time engaged at its work. He stands out before us as a neurotic case whose works are the result of a dislocated spirit. Frances Donaldson in her portrait of Evelyn Waugh as a country neighbour touches upon some such points of view as would go to prove to a considerable extent the causes of his creation of art. She explains very confidently how boredom and disgust are the motivating factors in the creation of his novels. She writes further to say that Evelyn Waugh would very often take a resort to the bromide and chloral as pain-killer—the result of which was the creation of *The Ordeal of Girbert Pinfold*. In the following passage, she gives a reliable portrait of Waugh's agonising sense of boredom at the question of a woman friend of his who said:

> Oh, Evelyn, I hear you've been ill. I hope you are better. "Evelyn burst into laughter and replied." I know that Laura has been putting it about that I've been ill. But it's not true. I've been off my head.[17]

But immediately afterwards Donaldson writes a very remarkable thing that must not escape our attention when she says:

> Evelyn was always tremendously diverted by the spectacle of someone making an ass of himself.

The feeling of 'someone making an ass of himself' seems to have derived from a complex Waugh has formed about himself. It is natural also for a man like Waugh to have such feeling in himself due to his over self-indulgence and pity the outcome of which is *The Ordeal of Gilbert Pinfold* which is very often termed as an autobiographical work of Evelyn Waugh. There is no doubt about this that these points give the impression of a man who has failed to adjust with the outside world due to his own personal idosyncrasies and propensities. It is on this very account that the following points of view recorded by Donaldson sound very much reliable and convincing:

> Evelyn suffered from a melancholia of Johnsonian proportions; and he found life so terribly boring he could hardly endure from day to day; he was often ill, seldom completely well; he was the only person I have ever known who seemed sincerely to long for death; he was terrifying to a stranger, merciless to a friend; but it's true his house and life revolved round jokes; very funny jokes.

We get the germs of truth in the above passage insofar as the revelation of Waugh's personality as a writer is concerned. It admits of little doubt that a man who "sufferes from a melancholia of Johnsonian proportions" and finds life so boring, whatever the reason, could be nothing short of a case of mental aberration. His leanings towards Roman Catholicism too seem to be the direct result of this mental disorder. One has to believe Donaldson again when she reports:

> Evelyn's books and his personality were the result of a kind of dislocation of spirit so violent that, if he joins the small

> body of artists whose work survives their lifetime, he will forever be a subject of speculation for biographers and psychologists.[18]

Waugh's personality as such becomes mysterious in itself and provokes biographers and psychologists both to speculate on this interesting issue. In this context, I would like to quote Evelyn Waugh himself who lays bare the secrets of his personality. He writes:

> Most of our forbears of whom we have any account have been hospitable and gregarious; my brother is all of that, retaining in his sixties an undiminished zest for form. I am easily bored and fond of solitude...precedent can be found in a few generations for every idiosyncrecy. The newspapers, I see, have now taken to the expression 'Genes' for what was once described as 'blood'. A happier metapher perhaps is a game of poker. Every card high and low, is in the pack of heredity. No two hands are idential.[19]

Waugh thus on the basis of this passage illustrates the significance of heredity presenting a clear-cut picture of his temperament dissimilar from that of Alec, his own brother. He appears then to be the best critic of himself besides remaining a permanent riddle for psychologists and speculators.

NOTES

1. Laurence Sterne. *The Making of a Humorist 1713-1762*. Margaret R.B. Shaw, London. The Richards Press, Royal Opera Arcade Pall Mall, 1957, p. 9.
2. *Critical Approaches to Literatures*. David Daiches. Longmans and Green and Co. London, New York, Toronto, pp. 340-43.
3. Evelyn Waugh. *Portrait of an Artist*. Fraderick J. Stopp, p. 11.
4. *Pertrait of an Artist*. Frederick J. Stopp, 1958. London Chapman and Hall, p. 12.
5. Frederick J. Stopp, p. 13.
6. *My Brother Evelyn and Other Profiles*. Alec Waugh Cassell. London 2nd Edition, January 1968, p. 165.
7. *When the Going was Good*. Evelyn Waugh, Penguin Book, 1968, p. 119.

8. Federick J. Stopp. *Portrait of an Artist*. 1958, London. Chapman and Hall, p. 19.

9. Stopp. *Portrait of an Artist*, p. 100. In 'Fanfare' (Life 1946, p. 90).

10. *My Brother Evelyn and Other Profiles*. Alec Waugh. Cessell London 1968. 2nd Edition, p. 192.

11. *Theory of Literature*, Rene Welleck and Austin Warren, p. 45.

12. *My Brother Evelyn and Other Profiles*, Alec Waugh. Cassell, London, 1968, pp. 166-67.

13. *Ibid.*, p. 163.

14. *Ibid.*, pp. 162-63.

15. "Temporary Officers and Gentlemen", John St. John. *The Sunday Times*. Sept. 7, 1969, p. 10.

16. *Ibid.*

17. Evelyn Waugh. *Portrait of a Country Neighbour*. Frances Donaldson. Printed in Great Britain by Coxt. Wyman Ltd., London, 1967, pp. 61-62.

18. Evelyn Waugh. *Portrait of a Country Neighbour*. Frances Donaldson. Introduction, p. 15.

19. *A Little Learning. The First Volume of an Autobiography*, Evelyn Waugh, p. 26.

5

CHAPTER

The Early Phase of Evelyn Waugh's Writing Career (1928-38)

A careful scrutiny of the career of Waugh from the beginning to the end would naturally lead one to a discussion of the various aspects of his novels, but chiefly character-delineation which (to my mind) seems to have formed the nucleus of the entire framework of his fiction. *Decline and Fall*, Waugh's first novel, is a concentrated study of Paul shown as developing through the horrible experiences of life. In fact, at the beginning Paul appears to be adorably innocent of the ugly realities of life, but later he has to plunge headlong into the deep ditches.

From the very early phase of his career. Waugh seems to be fully aware of the nuances of his characters. It is true that he might not appear mature enough at this early stage—in fact very few novelists are—yet a critic could hardly overlook this aspect of his artistic skill. The focus is on characters and one might easily trace out Waugh's indebtedness to the old masters, chiefly Fielding and Jane Austen. The main works of this period are *Decline and Fall* (1928), *Vile Bodies* (1930), *Black Mischief* (1932), *A Handful of Dust* (1934) and *Scoop* (1938). These five novels, one by one, seem to mark his growing interests in the eccentricities and idiosyncrasies of the Bright young People of the 1920s.

Decline and Fall

Decline and Fall is the first novel that established Waugh's reputation as a novelist of high promise. To quote Christopher Hollis:

With his first novel, *Decline and Fall*, published in 1928, Evelyn Waugh established his reputation as the novelist of the Bright Young Things of the 1920s. He established thus at one bound as one of the leading novelists of the day and maintained that reputation. At the same time, his talent like that of other novelists, perhaps sometimes had a little difficulty in persuading his admires to keep pace with his development.[1]

Decline and Fall is the study of a young man, Paul Penny Feather who is debagged by some rowdy boys at Oxford in the Bollinger Club and is made to come across ticklish situations after being sent down for his indecent behaviour. He faces the real world full of outward brightness and grandeur, becomes a school master at Llanabba Castle in North Wales and almost desperately lands into the sophisticated society of Mrs. Margo Best Chetwynde as her lover, who owns Latin American Entertainment Co. Ltd., as a den of brothels in South America. He is arrested, put into prison and is back at Oxford again to rejoin his former self. In the prison, he gets the chance of coming across characters like Captain Grimes, Solomon Philbrick and Prendergast, his former colleague and acquaintances, thus encountering several experiences of the outside world.

The novel starts with a scene of the annual dinner of Bollinger club consisting of characters from almost all walks of life. A portrait he draws here will be readily borne out by one who analyses the following description:

> At the last dinner, three years ago a fox had been brought in a cage and stoned to death with champagne bottles. What an evening that had been! This was the first meeting since then, and from all over Europe old members had rallied for the occasion. For two days they had been pouring into Oxford; Epileptic royalty from the villas of exile; uncouth peers from crumbling country seats, smooth young men of uncertain tastes from embassies and legations; illiterate lairds from wet granite hovels in the highlands; ambitious young barristers and conservative candidates from the London season and the indelicate advances of debutantes;

> all that was most sonorous of name and title was there for the beano.[2]

Examples of this kind of portraiture can be easily multiplied; but all these would reveal the novelist's insight into the trivial characters of the twenties and for that matter, his sure grasp of the very spirit of the age. His comic genius seems to lead him to present the oddities of the characters and thus make his novel a reliable and convincing portrait of life. He is a fine observer of the actions and morals of the Bright Young People forming different clubs of their own to entertain themselves. It should be clear from a careful scrutiny of the passage how very sarcastic Waugh's aims are and how very dispassionately he is assessing the sophisticated gathering that indulges in the fox-killing game with chamapagne bottles. It is in such an awful situation that Paul is made to figure, though surely he is doomed to cut a sorry figure. Naturally, he soon falls a prey to the rowdiness of his companions and has to suffer 'the slings and arrows of his outrangeous fortune.' The whole novel seems to be revolving round his characters, while other aspects of the novel, namely plot, dialogue, narrative technique and structure play only a subsidiary role. Character-delineation becomes the prime mover of the cycle of the novel. This might lead to a controversy in some quarters but one should admit the fact that Waugh is at his best while portraying a character.

The technique of Waugh is to present his character against the conflicting forces of society having their pulls and pressures in many directions. It is against the background of such conflicting forces that he allows them to have their acid test and hence the special importance of characterisation in his fiction. This should obviously highlight his freedom and flexibility in making a choice of the subject matter he seeks to deal with in his fiction. The following remark made by Miriam Allott would explain this point quite clearly:

> Two factors are of importance in affecting the novelist's solution of his technical difficulties; his own temperament and the nature of his subject. "Every great artist necessarily creates his own form," says Tolstoy in a statement which

> reads like a corollary to James's pronouncement about form and substance. Stevenson adds, "with each new subject... the true artist will vary his method and change the point of attack." This may superficially suggest that the novel is indeed as 'amorphous' as Mr. Forster says it is, but it seems true to say that the novelist's subject, 'method' and 'point of attack' produce a limited number of recognisable 'kinds'.[3]

In view of the above quotation, it would appear that Evelyn Waugh too with the help of his art of character-delineation determines the form and substance of his novel varying his method with each new subject. In other words, character-determination becomes the forte of the craft of his fictions enabling him to weigh and consider the world of mankind in general. It is natural on the part of his readers and critics alike to feel the forceful impact of the manners and morals of society on his sensibility. The very perspective of character thus provides him with a wide canvas of intellectual plane reflecting the spirit of his time. Prendergast's criticism of the justification of God's creation of this world gives a convincing portrait of the scepticism of the time when he gives vent to his feeling:

> Yes, I've not known an hour's real happiness since. You see, it wasn't the ordinary sort of Doubt about Cain's wife or the Old Testament miracles or the consecration of Archbishop Parker. I'd been taught now to explain all those while I was at college. No, it was something deeper than all that. I couldn't understand why God had made the world at all. There was my mother and Bundles and Mrs. Grump talking away quite unconcernedly while I sat there wrestling with this sudden assault of doubt. You see how fundamental that is. Once granted the first step, I can see that everything else that follows—Tower of Babel. Babylonian captivity, Incarnation, Church, Bishops, incense, everything—but what I couldn't see now, is, why did it all begin?[4]

Waugh is an adept in the art of characterisation indeed. His main interest seems to consist in pointing out the diverse aspects of a character explaining through him thus the prevailing spirit of his time. To quote Martin Turnell in this context explaining the value of character in fiction:

> A character is a verbal construction which has no existence outside the book. It is a vehicle for the novelist's sensibility and its significance lies in its relations with the author's other constructions. A novel is essentially a verbal pattern in which the different "characters" are strands and the reader's experience is the impact of the complete pattern on his sensibility.[5]

It admits of little doubt on the basis of the above observation how the aspect of characterisation becomes the corner-stone of Waugh's fiction making other aspects subsidiary in their importance.

At the same time, a scrutiny of the early phase of Waugh's career should help one determine his comic genius which gives an ample proof of the principle that characterisation is the only appropriate device to enable one to be a comedian. It seems as if Waugh could hardly have been a comic writer, had be not shown his deep interest in studying the minute aspects of the Bright Young People of the twenties. For example, who would not be impressed by the note of irony Waugh seems to be using in delineating the portrait of Margot whom Paul shields from the consequences of her crimes as a white slaver accepting imprisonment?

> As he studied Margot's photograph dubiously transmitted as it was, he was strengthened in his belief that there was, in fact, and should be one law for her and another for himself, and that the raw little exertions of nineteenth-century Radicals were essentially base and trival and misdirected. It was not simply that Margot had been very rich or that he had been in love with her. It was just that he saw the impossibility of Margot in prison; the bare connection of vocables associating the ideas was obscene.[6]

Decline and Fall thus bears the stamp of Waugh's creative imagination dealing with his "method of mixing farce, comedy of character and satire and telling his story with that studied understatement of the shocking which relates him more closely to the deepened manner of Damon Runyon than to the self-conscious seaminess of the early Huxley or the mannered violence of Hemingway."[7]

Vile Bodies (1930), written during the very early phase of his career, is a by-product of the same rich sensibility. It is another example of his comic wit and character-delineation. His real aim of writing fiction, as he himself discloses, "has been to distill comedy and sometimes tragedy from the knockabout farce of peoples' outward behaviour."[8] Judged in this light, *Vile Bodies* portrays the outward behaviour of his characters showing his keen interest in their affairs and actions. It presents a fine study of the cleavage between the values of life represented on the one hand by the young and the old on the other. The photography of the morals and manners of society this time gains in-depth and variety. Besides, the very perspective of the individual and society seems to be widening which leads him to a minute analysis of the varied shades of human character.

Vile Bodies tells the story of Adam Symes and Nina who appear just at the beginning of the novel. They are restless to marry each other but unfortunately a curious mixture of events takes place foiling their plan completely. As a consequence of the untoward happenings, Nina marries Ginger, a rich young man, but Adam cuckolds him (Ginger) ingeniously by pretending to be Nina's husband (by impersonating Ginger) on a Christmas visit to Nina's home. In the meanwhile, the war breaks out interrupting this idyll and the story comes to an end with Adam reading a letter from Nina in the midst of 'the biggest battlefield in the history of the world'.

A careful examination of the different aspects of the novel illustrates this point clearly as to how the two things—comic strain and character-delineation above all dominate the mind of readers and critics alike. Waugh, if clearly observed, seems to be growing more and more witty and sarcastic in his vein and mode of writing. It is on account of this characteristic that his portrayal of character becomes much more important than any other aspect of his fiction. His characters bear their individual traits as a result of which they are called Chastity, Humility, Prudence, Divine Discontent, respectively representing thus their creator's wit and humour. The portrait of passengers making their voyage is worth-quoting when he paints them with the brush of his wit and humour:

> Of the other passengers, some had filled their ears with cotton-wool, others wore smoked glasses, while several ate dry captain's biscuits from paper bags, as Red Indians are said to eat snake's flesh to make them cunning.[9]

Not merely that, the picture of Adam Symes, the hero of the novel is also worthnoting:

> Two minutes before the advertised time of departure, while the first admonitory whistling and sounding was going on, a young man came to board carrying his bag. There was nothing particularly remarkable about his appearance. He looked exactly as young men like him to look; he was carrying his own bag which was disagreeably heavy, because he had no money left in francs and very little left in anything else.[10]

Waugh's aim in the passages quoted above is to strike the note of healthy humour which not only relaxes one's mind but also provokes one to think more and more minutely about the actions and attitudes of the characters moving in society. Like a cartoonist with the help of his words he creates a sense of ridicule and laughter making them (characters) lifelike and convincing. One could be easily struck by the funny picture of father Rothschilde, a jesuit priest who is behaving in an unnatural and unseemly way. The portrayal of such characters reminds one of the master-craftsmen like Fielding and Jane Austen who have created miracles by the appropriate use of words in their appropriate context. One could hardly restrain one's laughter at the witty portrait of Father Rothschilde who is moving on the deck of the ship with a suitcase containing "some rudimentary underclothes, six important new books in six languages, a false beard and a school atlas and gazetter heavily annotated." The picture of his tongue protruding slightly is also no less thought-provoking which resembles as Waugh describes, "those plaster reproductions of the gargoyles of Notre Dame which may be seen in the shop windows of artists colourmen tinted in colour of 'Old Ivory' peering intently from among stencil outfits and plasticine and tubes of water-colour paint."[11]

The picture of Father Rothschilde reminds one of Mr. Collins in Jane Austen's *Pride and Prejudice* who is an object of laughter and ridicule in much the same way. Waugh's art of characterisation thus seems to be based on his correct observation of the varied facets of one's personality. It is on account of these qualities that Quentin Blake in his cover illustration passes the following remarks about this novel:

> The scene and climate of this witty, satirical novel give full scope to Evelyn Waugh's sardonic observation. Here again, as in *Decline and Fall*, we are in the fashionable Mayfair of the twenties, when the Bright young things exercised their inventive minds (and *Vile Bodies*) in every kind of capricious escapade. The plot is an adroit jigsaw of amusing situations; the characters a vivid assortment of those who inhabit the social domain that lies between Park Lane and Bond Street.[12]

In Waugh's fiction, if minutely observed, the subjective and objective observation both get merged together and the fusion of both the elements of life—outer and inner, private and public gives rise to the emergence of characters in his fiction. He seems to be thus chiming with the views of Nancy Hale who holds:

> There are of course two sources of characters in fiction-outside observation and the various aspects of oneself. In either case the process of the creation of a character in fiction is almost wholly subjective, so that these two sources for ideas for characters inevitably become merged.... In either case, elements of both real, outer life and inner, private life are put into the smeltery of the creative process, where, as so many writers express it, they cook before emerging as a new thing, a character.[13]

Black Mischief (1932), written during the early period of his career as a novelist is a brilliant study of characters. Waugh here studies the politics of an Abyssinia—like African Island whose emperor Seth foists the customs of 'modern progress' on his barbarous subjects against their will, being aided and abetted in the realisation of this aim by Basil Seal, a perverted genius of the time. Basil Seal happens to have been as a matter of coincidence his old friend at Oxford during their college days. Being so, he

(Basil) takes Seth into confidence with whose help he (Seth) introduces scientific theories of radical reforms—town planning from Paris, a Museum and a penal reform, clothes from Europe, Nackt-Kultur from Berlin so as to modernise Africa. All his attempts at modernising Africa however ultimately boomerang at him giving rise to a revolt by the local elements leading to his assassination.

With the help of these characters, Waugh makes a successful study of the politics of an Abyssinia-like African island simmering with discontent and resentment at the sight of forced introduction of foreign reforms hardly suiting the taste of the native population. It is thus a concentrated study of two different cultures diametrically opposed to each other in their essence and spirit. Waugh seems to be ridiculing the enthusiastic wave of humanism which seeks to transform the whole society but is actuated by the feeling of black mischief resulting in the coup d'état led by Seth's own men who kill him.

It is, as it appears, a minute study of the character of the European civilization which Waugh seems to be making ingeniously through Basil Seal, Dame Mildred and Miss Sarah Tin—the representatives of modern culture. Characters are thus the media through whom he presents a concentrated study of the complexity of modern civilization. Black Mischief thus marks a further landmark of progress in his keen study of a complex society which is full of vicious people like Basil Seal, Dame Mildred Perch and Miss Sarah Tin. The sarcastic portrait of Seth, the blind follower of modern progress, is beautifully drawn by Waugh when he makes an indirect attack at his belief in progress:

> I have been to Europe—I have read modern books—Shaw, Arlen Priestley...at my stirrups runs woman's suffrage, vaccination and vivisection. I am the New Age. I am the Future.[14]

Waugh's abstract world immediately takes a concrete shape as soon as he starts treating his characters sarcastically with a view to exposing their hollowness from within. Their speech as a result of this satiric touch seems to be full of sound and fury signifying nothing ultimately. His characters as such stand out on familiar grounds often reminding us of Dr. Johnson's remarks about Shakespeare that his characters are the common species of mankind inheriting their common weaknesses. "The novel", says Malcolm Bradbury, "creates, but never finally resolves a condition of equipoise between the progressive and modern and the barbarian and primitive. Our sympathies never go out wholly either to Seal or to Seth."[15]

Waugh's comic integrity finds its concrete expression in this novel and he employs his wit and humour excellently by producing a note of irony. To quote Christopher Hollis for a vivid and clear realisation of the gravity of the novel *Black Mischief*:

> All that here is satirised and attacked is insincerity. Seth had brought back from Europe no understanding of anything but its absurdities. Professor Toynbee in our own days has told us how much earlier it is to spread rapidly the superficial techniques of European civilization than it is to spread its spiritual essence—and how much more dangerous—and the evidence of this danger we can see clearly around us. Waugh said it all a great deal more amusingly than Professor Toynbee and twenty years before him.[16]

A Handful of Dust (1934) is a tour-de-force of this period which bears distinct signs of the maturity of Waugh's mind and art. Here one marks a note of difference in his attitude to his characters which is his psychological probe into their inner consciousness. Up to this stage he seems to have described the outward mood and behaviour of his characters but now his interest takes an admirable turn making him peep into the inner substratum of one's personality. It is in one way a voyage within rather than without that becomes the principal concern of his artistic sensibility.

A Handful of Dust is the study of a broken marriage. Tony Last and Brenda, a married couple, can't adjust with each other because of their attitudes to life being dissimilar in nature. Tony Last unlike his wife Brenda feels satisfied with the rural life in the Victorian Gothic mansion. Naturally, Brenda feeling bored with the dull surrounding of the Gothic mansion makes up her mind to stay in a flat in London enjoying the pleasures of city life. She then falls in love with Beaver, a merchant and during her absence from the Gothic mansion she, as ill luck would have it, loses her only son John Andrews coming under the cruel feet of a horse. As a result of this tragedy, she feels her relationship with Tony Last to have been completely cut-off and being thus indifferent to him gives him divorce. The ties of marriage are thus broken completely reducing their life almost to a non-entity. Brenda files a suit for her maintenance amount in the court; gets it but makes her life torn and bruised. Even Beaver, the merchant who had given her temptations of many kinds leaves her in the lurch. Tony on the other hand gets frustrated and goes out of Hetton in search of a city with Dr. Messinger and comes to Brazil where he is imprisoned by Mr. Todd, a villager who asks him (Tony) to read Dickens aloud and ultimately dies there.

Whatever the story be, *A Handful of Dust* is a deep study of the inner workings of the minds of Tony Last and Brenda. The novel seems to be based on the tragic conception of Shakespeare: 'character is destiny' is out and out a concentrated study of characters in their actions and reactions to the vicious circumstances of life moulding their destiny. At this stage, it appears as if Waugh has grown very much inquisitive to know the how and why of the function of a human brain and its mysterious reactions to certain situations in life. It is, however, the objective detachment of Evelyn Waugh that draws one's attention here. Waugh does not seem to be sympathising with either Brenda or Tony Last in spite of their lives being tragic. This sort of objective detachment reminds one of great humorists like Fielding, Dickens and Jane Austen. To quote Tony Evans for a full clarifications of this point of view:

> Evelyn Waugh is too subtle a moralist, however, to point a moral and leaves his readers to take what side they will in this story of a broken marriage. He is, moreover, too sophisticated a chronicler to ignore the comic and the ridiculous in human misfortune, and a Handful of Dust is well-flavoured with his shrewd and astringent humour.[17]

One might thus mark a note of emotional hardness in him towards his characters because of his impartiality. The following extract from the text is enough to suggest this note:

> "Was anyone hurt?"
>
> No one, I am thankful to say, said Mrs. Beaver, except two house-maids who lost their heads and jumped through a glass roof into the paved court. They were in no danger.[18]

Here Waugh should appear to be a successful painter of the absurdities, eccentricities and whimsicalities of modern civilization which in its frenzied excitement has created a laughable stock of characters acting in an idiosyncratic manner. The novel confirms the view of Waugh that his main aim of writing fiction "has been to distill comedy and sometime tragedy from the knockabout farce of peoples' outward behaviour." The note of his realism then is at once 'comic and grim' as it has been pertinently pointed out by Walter Allen:

> Fantasy disappears altogether in *A Handful of Dust* (1934). Here we are in the real world and innocence is well and truly done down. At once comic and grim, *A Handful of Dust* is one of the best novels of our time. Contempt for the social scene depicted and for those who inhabit it has entered in, and so has bitterness. It is a story of the destruction of Tony Last by his wife Brenda, a destruction motivated not by malignance, indeed scarcely motivated at all, but the outcome of boredom and irresponsible selfishness.[19]

It is amply clear from the above passage that like Fielding and Jane Austen, Waugh does not merely make an attempt to expose the superficialities of his characters only, but goes on to look beneath these trivialities too. It is on account of this attitude that Waugh's fiction besides being 'Comic' is grim in content and ends as a highly moving piece. His vision does not fail him in finding out terror even in a handful of dust. Waugh is in a far more advantageous position than Fielding, Dickens and Jane Austen insofar as the exploration of the inner functioning of one's brain is concerned owing to the advancement of modern psychology at the hands of Freud and Jung. He thus seems to be even surpassing his masters as such in the art of fiction-writing.

Bradbury also does not miss to trace out the intermixture of farce with seriousness in *A Handful of Dust* when he holds:

> Farce is intermixed with seriousnss in such a fashion as to turn the book in another direction and there is a deep ambivalence in Waugh's approach which prevents us from accepting unreservedly the aristocratic myth with which he is associated. In this sense Last anticipates Guy Crouchback.[20]

A Handful of Dust is thus a brilliant achievement of Evelyn Waugh which hints at the unusual depth and profundity he seems to be aiming at in this novel.

Scoop (1938) is another novel of this period which is done round a reliable and convincing portrait of the world of journalism in a comic vein. It is the story of William Boot, an innocent man who contributes to the newspaper *Beast* his description of 'lush places' in finding out terror in its bi-weekly half-column devoted to Nature. He is by some mistaken identity of his distant cousin John Boot sent to Ishmaelia to cover events of journalistic importance. He, however, is completely ignorant of the sophisticated art of journalism and cuts a very sorry figure there in the midst of correspondents coming from different places. He does not send any valuable piece of news to the press in England waiting anxiously for it to scoop the whole world. Being innocent by nature, he happens to fall in love with Katchen, the wife of a German speculator. It is she who supplies him with a bag of stones for f20 and a startling news that Ishmaelia is in the grip of a crisis due to a keen competition going on between Russia and Germany for acquiring the gold-ore. It is this very sensational news that William Boot sends to Lord Copper, the proprietor of the British newspaper who by publishing it scoops the whole world of journalism at one stoke. Boot as a result of the publication of this startling news is at once rewarded knighthood, which however is received by one John Boot, an urban novelist due to the mistaken identity of the genuine William Boot, a country side correspondent contributing his description of the 'hush places' to the newspaper *Beast*.

Finally, it is the superb handling of plot and character that renders this novel striking. It becomes all the more interesting when one follows the curious mixture of events having their bearings on the development of plot. It appears to be the novelist's primary purpose to underline the important role of chances playing their part in the life of man. The mistaken identity of both the Boots is in itself an interesting event. Thus Waugh proves it quite admirably how chances come to play their amusing role in one's life. The case of the substitution of 'great-crested grebe' by Priscila for 'badger' throughout the manuscript of a recent article on Lush Places (that enables William Boot to get a chance to go to London at the summons of Lord Copper) is equally interesting. But the real significance of the plot of the novel may be missed for want of a careful study of the nuances of characters like William Boot and John Boot and Mr. Salter. The portrait of the William Boot, a correspondent from the countryside as contrasted with the urban journalists is undoubtedly interesting and witty in significance. He is a simpleton knowing little about the skill and tact of journalism. It is because of this little knowledge of journalism that he acts foolishly in the company of a large gathering of sophisticated correspondents at Ishmaelia till he secures a sensational item of news from Katchen and sends it to the British press. By juxtaposing the character-sketches of William Boot and Mr. Salter, a foreign correspondent, one could easily get an insight into the contrasting aspects of their character. Waugh's rendering of the contrast is noteworthy:

> It was an encounter of great embarrassment for both of them. For William it was the hour of retribution; he advanced, heavy with guilt to meet whatever doom had been decreed for him. Mr. Salter had the more active part. He was under orders to be cordial and spring Lord Copper's proposal on the poor hick when he had won his confidence by light conversation and heavy hospitality.... His knowledge of real life was meagre.... Normal life, as he saw it, consisted in regular journeys by electric train, monthly cheques, communal amusements and a cosy horizon of states and chimneys; there was something un-English and not quite right about 'the country' with its solitude and self-sufficiency, its bloody recreations, its darkness and silence and suden,

> inexplicable noises; the kind of place where you never knew from one minute to the next that you might not be tossed by a bull or pitch-forked by a Yokel or rolled over and broken up by a pack of hounds.[21]

Also, the aforesaid passage is a clear-cut illustration of the serio-comic attitude of Waugh to his characters which puts him in the gallery of great ironists like Shaw, Fielding and Jane Austen.

Scoop thus is the last work of this fertile period which presents a light and detached treatment of his comic attitude to his characters. Mr. 'Bradbury's remark on this novel is an ideal summing up:

> *Scoop* is high farce and abounds in burlesque passages, mistaken identities, stylised misunderstanding, characters simplified and heightened in comic proportions. It in no way engages the reader in such sympathies as *A Handful of Dust* has required, and though there is some similarity of material—once again there are two worlds, an agrarian and associated with a country house, the other metropolitan and international and associated with a London changing yet further into a city of demolition and traffic jaws—the treatment is lighter, more detached.[22]

The early phase of Waugh's career as a novelist is thus a sound proof of the skilful handing of characters gaining in depth and maturity all the more in the middle phase of his development as a writer of fiction.

NOTES

1. *Evelyn Waugh*. Christopher Hollis, Published for the British Council by Longman Group Ltd., 1971, p. 5.
2. Prelude. *Decline and Fall*. Evelyn Waugh. Penguin Series, p. 9.
3. *Novelists on the Novel*. Miriam Allott. Third Impression, 1960. Routledge and Kegan Paul Ltd., p. 164.
4. *Decline and Fall*, Evelyn Waugh, p. 33.
5. Martin Turnell. *The Novel in France* (1950), p. 6 (taken from Novelist's on the Novel-Miriam Allott, p. 198).

6. *Decline and Fall.* Evelyn Waugh, p. 188.
7. Frederick J. Stopp. *Evelyn Waugh: Portrait of an Artist*, 1958, p. 64.
8. Evelyn Waugh.
9. *Vile Bodies*, E. Waugh. Penguin Series, 1967, pp. 12-13.
10. *Ibid.*
11. *Ibid.*, p. 9.
12. *Vile Bodies.* Penguin Series, 1967. Cover illustration by Quentin Blake.
13. *The Realities of Fiction*, Nancy Hale, London, Macmillan & Co. Ltd., 1963, p. 49.
14. Black Mischief, *Evelyn Waugh*, p. 17.
15. *Evelyn Waugh* by Malcolm Bradbury, Edinburgh and London, 1964, pp. 53-54.
16. *Evelyn Waugh* by Christopher Hollis, Published for the British Council by Longman Group Ltd., 1971, p. 10.
17. *A Handful of Dust.* Penguin Series. 1968, Cover illustration by Tony Evens.
18. *A Handful of Dust*, E. Waugh, p. 7.
19. Tradition and Dream, Walter Allen. The English and American Novel from the Twenties to our time. Phoenix House London, 1964, p. 210.
20. *Evelyn Waugh* by Malcolm Bradbury. Edinburgh and London, 1964, pp. 53-54.
21. *Scoop*, Evelyn Waugh, Penguin Series, pp. 26-27.
22. *Evelyn Waugh*, Malcolm Bradbury, Edinburgh and London, 1964, p. 68.

6

CHAPTER

The Middle Phase of Evelyn Waugh's Writing Career (1934-50)

In the middle phase of his career as a novelist, Waugh appears to have made a definite advance on his earlier accomplishment with regard to both mind and art. As soon as one reaches this stage of his artistic development, one finds a marked change in his outlook and also in his responses and reactions to the period he lives in. Here one must underline an important fact of biography that he was passing through a series of some such circumstances as were bound to have the impact upon his sense and sensibility and for that matter on his life and art. The early phase of his career was a phase of apprenticeship in the art and technique of novel-writing but during the middle phase one can easily note a new slant, a new stance in his attitude to life. His personal life also seems to have suffered a setback in the sudden death of his father along with the change and decay all around due to the outbreak of the Second World War. Earlier, he had dealt with the social themes in a spirit of levity which now under the stress of the difficult times he just could not afford. The mood of the artist that emerges out of the fight he seems determined to put up is marked by disillusionment and bitterness. The comic vein still persists, but now it undergoes a mark of distinction in method and style. The art of characterisation, however, improves considerably and it seems, as if his views about the importance of characters were similar to the views of Nancy Hale who holds:

> I don't think there can be any question but what characters, characters that seem to live, are the most important single element in the novel. No one remembers novels for their style, or for the skill with which their plots were constructed. What we remember is princess Marya and Prince Andrei; Becky Sharp and Lady Dedlock, Zuleika Dobson and Lewis Eliot's neurotic wife Sheila. Characters, characters that have a universal appeal; are, in fact, the life of a novel or a short story.[1]

Observed in view of the passage, quoted above, it would appear that we remember Evelyn Waugh too for the creation of Guy Crouckback, Basil Seal, Paul, Charles Ryder and many others more than any other thing in his novel for their universal appeal.

Work Suspended (1942), *Put Out More Flags* (1942), *Brideshead Revisited* (1945), *The Loved One* (1948), and *Helena* (1950) are supposed to be the important works of this period.

Work Suspended, an unfinished novel of this period, seems to have been written in an autobiographical vein. It is natural on this ground to witness a marked change in Waugh's art of narrative technique which replaces the use of the third person by the use of the first person. This change in the art of writing is remarkable from the point of view of the element of sentiment entering spontaneously the realm of his fiction.

Work Suspended narrates the story of John Plant, a writer of detective stories who lives in a small hotel in Fez. He often pays his formal visits to the large house in St. John's Wood to see his father residing there. Plant Senior, his father, a great classical painter and Royal Academician meets with an accident at the hands of Arthur Atwater, a commercial traveller, being run over by his car. 'A religious ceremony of an unostentatious kind' is done at the hands of his uncle Andrew but he does not like to stay at St. John's Wood giving him little peace of mind. He goes to London at the summons of the court to plead for his father against Arthur Atwater, the slayer of his father; compromises with him and starts a fresh lease of life. He starts an affair with

Lucy, the wife of a friend and fellow writer, Roger Simmonds, violating thus an essential modesty and solitude. Lucy delivers a child on the 25 August 1939 and with the siren sound of the air-raid, giving a false alarm of the Second World War, the novel remains unfinished and ends.

The novel, in spite of having remained unfinished, bears the stamp of the novelist's creative imagination. It is for the first time in his career as a novelist that Waugh considers biography to be a rich source of artistic inspiration. Not merely that; in the matter of character-delineation, a deep understanding and insight into the emotions and feelings of an individual seems to have developed. As a matter of fact, 'sentiment' and 'sensibility' both undergo a curious metamorphosis in view of his personal reactions and attitudes to life. He seems to be over-whelmed with self-pity that gives a vent to his nostalgic feelings making his works a bit serious in tone and significance. It would be apt to refer to the sentimental picture of Plant senior, drawn by Evelyn Waugh thus:

> There are only three classes in England now—politicians, tradesmen and slaves.... Seventy years ago the politicians and the tradesmen were in alliance; they destroyed the gentry by destroying the value of land; some of the gentry became politicians themselves, others tradesmen; out of what was left they created a new class into which I was born, the moneyless, landless educated gentry who managed the country for them. My grandfather was a canon of Christ Church, my father was in the Bengal service. All the capital they left their sons was education and moral principle. Now the politicians are in alliance with the slaves to destroy the tradesmen. They don't need to bother us. We are extinct already. "I am a Dodo," he used to say definitely staring at his audience. "You, my poor son, are a petrified egg."[2]

By perusing these words we come across a different Waugh moving in the context of different circumstances that mould the pattern of his fiction-writing. He appears to be sober and grave in his response to the painful circumstances of life. He does not however, give up his wit and humour although the note of asringency is noteceable here. The art of characterisation (owing to this factor) gains in depth and meaning hinting thus at the further growth of his mind and art. The portrait of Lucy drawn here is worth appreciating when contrasted with the simplicity and innocence of Wordsworth's Lucy. Waugh's Lucy is of an urban surrounding representing a natural animalism characterised by Humboldt's Gibbon, a creature which Lucy and Plant both happen to see at the London zoo. Naturally, it requires a different presentation at his hands. To quote Malcolm Bradbury:

> This requires a new presentation. In the earlier novels social delineation, though accurately and sharply given, is subordinate to fantasy; here and in later novels this is reversed. Thus while the earlier novels lend, so to speak, to start from the world of anarchy and put to the test the world of order, the later ones lend rather to start from order and judge anarchy in terms of it. The myth of the past begins to grow, to appear in the novels as an ideal prelapsarian world, but it would be wrong to suggest that Waugh is fictionally entirely committed to it.[3]

From the fictional point of view thus *Work Suspended* marks the growth of Waugh's sensibility. It seems to be a journey of his artistic career from the world of innocence to the world of experience. Naturally then, the artistic output of this middle period is not merely entertaining and sense-exciting, but thought-provoking too in a social, political, moral and intellectual sense. To quote Frederick J. Stopp:

> The two chapters of an unfinished novel published in 1942 as *Work Suspended* have an importance out of all proportion to their length. The plot is not, as in the entertainments primarily farcial or burlesque; the central figure neither an innocent nor a bounder, but capable of development; the story is told in the first person.[4]

Put Out More Flags is the print of this very fertile period which deals with a background of phoney war popularly termed as the Great Bore War. Published in 1942, the novel portrays the complete chaotic situation ushered in by the Second World

War. It is, mainly speaking, a concentrated study of the character of Basil Seal, the rogue here of the period who exploits the deteriorating situation of the period to his own advantage and grinds his axe without caring for any scruples. He represents the attributes of an anti-hero deviating completely from the conventional path of morality and virtue. War to him is a blessing in disquise which makes him to one's utter surprise fish in troubled waters of the period. His chief aim is to make profit by hook or by crook. To realise this aim he sells a family of slum children called the Connollys and tricks Ambrose Silk, his fast friend into writing a Fascist pamphlet getting him thus arrested by police on the charge of treason. He is an adept in the art of eave-teasing taking thus a malicious pleasure in the company of girls.

Waugh, as a novelist, seems to be attaining a height of perfection in this middle period of his career. His brain is reaching a stage of maturity resulting in the creation of such sensational fiction. In his dedicatory letter to Sir Winston Churchill he writes that he deals "mostly, with a race of ghosts, the survivors of the world we both knew ten years ago, which you have outflown in the empyrean of strenuous politics, but where my imagination still fondly lingers. I find more food for thought in the follies of Basil Seal and Ambrose Silk, than in the sagacity of the higher command. These characters are no longer contemporary in sympathy; they were forgotten even before the war; but they lived on delightfully in holes and corners and, like everyone else, they have been disturbed in their habits by the rough intrusion of current history. Here they are in that odd, dead period before the Churchillian renaissance which people called at the time the Great Bore War."[5]

The work seems to be written in the nature of a dark comedy of the Shakespearean kind. The art of characterisation consequently gains immensely in significance which is clearly reflected in the following portrait of Basil Seal in the words of Barbara, his sister:

> You know exactly what I mean. Basil needed a war. He is not meant for peace.[6]

It is an exciting portrait of Basil Seal that often challenges one's usual conception of man. A few further details of his character present his portrait more clearly and vividly when Waugh himself mentions about him:

> He was used in his life to a system of push, appeasement agitation and blackmail, which except that it had no more distant aim than his own immediate amusement ran parallel to Nazi diplomacy.[7]

Waugh's art of characterisation appears to be gaining gradually though surely in depth, variety, polish and brilliance.

Ambrose Silk's character-sketch on the other hand is all the more attractive and admirable. He possesses the attributes of an intellectual 'pining for what is not, beating his luminous wings as it were in a void'. One might well mark the inensity of his grief at the sad plight of intellectuals preferring the company of ranks to that of their fellows.

Put Out More Flags—thus from the point of view of art, draws an admirable picture of the conflicting ideologies of collectivism and individualism illustrated in the characters of Basil Seal and Ambrose Silk, respectively. In course of discussing the worth of this novel one could hardly miss the value of the unforgettable words of Ambrose Silk presenting an admirable analysis of the culture of the present age that has ceased to be conventual and acquired a cenobitic character. To quote Cedric's words, while fighting in the battlefield:

> The great weapons of modern war did not count in single lines; it took a whole section to make a target with a burst of machine gun-fire, a platoon or a motor lorry to be worth a tomb...divided we stand, united we fall, thought cedric.... He did not know it, but he was thinking exactly what Ambrose had thought when he announced that culture must cease to be conventual and become cenobitic.[8]

Put Out More Flags is thus an outcome of Waugh's developed sense and sensibility. He seems to be at his best here while attempting to give a lively photograph of his characters. It is characterisation alone that engages one's attention here which often appears to be transgressing the limits of common sense and imagination. Christopher Hollis's comments seem to be quite pertinent in this context when he holds:

> The trouble with Basil Seal is that, if we consider him a real character, he is too odious to be funny. Had he been content to remain a character in one of Waugh's earlier novels such as *Decline and Fall*—in a fantastic world of fantastic people—we could have laughed at him as a mere formula of villainy without any attempt to pass a moral judgement on a person. We can tolerate him even in *Azania*. But in a real world, alongside real and suffering people at a great crisis of our history, he is too horrible.[9]

Hollis's comments, however do not damage Waugh's reputation but increase it in view of his creative imagination that could give shape to a character like Basil Seal even.

Waugh here in his art of characterisation does not seem to be in any way inferior to Bernard Shaw drawing a mock-heroic picture of the world he deals with in his play. One could be easily confirmed of this fantastic pursuit when one compares Basil Seal with Sergius regarding the mock-heroic attitude to military life:

> "For Basil Seal," writes Frederick J. Stopp, "reality falls short of the ideal. His fantasy of military glory is not that of a subaltern in a trench at zero hour, but that of receiving a top secret assignment from a lean, scarred man with hard grey eyes' at an obscure address in Maida Vale."

Brideshead Revisited, a novel written in 1945 seeks to deal with a common religious theme of good and evil against the Catholic background of the Brideshead Castle. In the words of Waugh himself, its theme is "the operation of divine grace on a group of diverse but closely connected characters". It is on account of this that one becomes suspicious about his real intention in writing this novel. Whatever the intention be, the novel is eschatological in character and theme and happens to be a grand success from the point of view of the art of fiction-writing. It is in the author's own words "Offered to a younger generation of readers as a souvenir of the Second War rather than of the twenties or of the thirties with which it ostensibly deals."

It is the story of one Charles Ryder whose sacred and profane memories of Brideshead, the house of the Flyte family, during his sojourn there at the time of the Second World War, inspire him to write the story of the decline and fall of this family. He narrates the story as to how in close association he had lived with this family and come to know Sebastian, Julia, Cordelia, Lady Marchmain, Bridey and Rex Mortram, the members of the family. The memories of the golden past when he was reading with Sebastian in Oxford and Lord Marchmain who had come back to the Brideshead Castle to breathe his last, after having spent the major portion of his life with Cara, his mistress and the insistence on the part of Julia Marchmain to marry Rex Mortrain against the wishes of Lady Marchmain on the grounds of his religion and his having kept a mistress provide him with a storehouse of treasured memories which he as a dispassionate observer now remembers. Besides he reports how the Protestant religion ultimately gives a green signal to both of them to marry each other but their conjugal life becomes unhappy due to Rex's avarice for her money.

Evelyn Waugh is at his best here as a practitioner of fiction-writing. The delineation of character is almost on the verge of perfection. Nowhere else do we come across such full-length size of characters as drawn in *Brideshead Revisited*. The broadness of vision, the sense of maturity, the gravity of tone and purpose seem to be gaining in their superiority for the first time in this novel.

The three-dimensional growth of fiction is for the first time seen in full perspective in this novel. The most impressive phenomenon to be observed here, as it seems to be, is the happy blending of romance and realism, the seen and the unseen and the far and the near which bears the sign and the mark of fullness and maturity on the part of a growing artist like Waugh. It is a successful study of a divided house in the wake of the deteriorating morals and values of a war-torn society having its inescapable impact on the mind of a young generation. Waugh makes a minute study of the deterioration of these values in the presentation of characters like Julia and Rex Mortran determined to flout the wishes of Lady Marchmain on the issue of their marriage, becoming a controversial issue in view of the rites and customs of the Flyte family represented by Lady Marchmain. It is on this ground that Waugh seems to be fully justified in making the captain Charles Ryder recollect the sacred and profane memories of the Brideshead Castle. The brilliant execution of this novel is clearly pointed out by De Vitis in the following manner when he holds:

> The novel is brilliantly conceived and brilliantly executed. The integration of plot, character and action with the theme denotes the most competent artistry. It is, wrong, I think to condemn the novel as flagrantly romantic, as Edmund Wilson does, or to insist that romantic adolescence is "Waugh's only touchstone of significance of human existence" and therefore indequate, as D.S. savage does.... It's true that there are elements which at times intrude—Waugh's snobbery and his pre-occupation with the aristocracy make themselves uncomfortably apparent. But the impression the novel makes is a universal and valid one because it does deal with the real world convincingly.[10]

Judged on the basis of the above observation, the novel *Brideshead Revisited* seems to be an example of Waugh's creditable achievement from the point of view of the art of fiction-writing. It is the age itself that is clearly reflected through characterisation in the novel. There is hardly any character conceived here in an unconvincing and unfaitherful detail and as such there is an admirable touch of proximity and nearness with them. For example, let us refer to the character-sketch of Rex Mortram:

> Oh, Rex's parties! Politics and money. They can't do anything except for money, if they walk round the lake they have to make bets about how many swans they see...sitting up till two amusing Rex's girls, hearing them gossip, rattling away endlessly on the backgammon board while the men play cards and smoke cigars.[11]

The novel is manifestly a fine portrait of the age which it mirrors so successfully as if the camera of his imagination were photographing the age as it is rather than as it should be. It marks the subdued laughter of Evelyn Waugh unlikely to be found in the early phase of his career. Waugh terms the novel as an 'apologia' on account of the conspicuous absence of this element in this novel but a careful diagnosis of the work would reveal this element arising from a great variety of causes which are very often found in the case of our analysis of comedy as a whole. To quote J.L. Styan in support of this view:

> The diagnosis of comedy presents many difficulties. Laughter, a recurring and therefore an evidently important ingredient, seems to arise from a great variety of sources: We laugh at other people's bad luck, or at relief from embarrassment, or at a little flattery, or even when we do not want to laugh. We laugh heartily, or smile gently, or at some comedy we may not laugh at all. There are so many uses to which laughter can be put, from the promotion of a cold vindictive sarcasm to that of the empty gaiety of knockabout.[12]

Scott King's Modern Europe, another famous work of this period, narrates a sad story of a classical scholar who, getting an invitation from Neutralia to recite the verses of Bellorius, attends the function there (Neutralia), but to his utter surprise he finds the people there taking little interest in Bellorius and indulging themselves in cheap-graded politics of regaining the lost international reputation of Neutralia instead. He faces a grave situation when his host falls from power due to the vicious circle of politics and flees away from there for his life. It is here again that one could easily find Waugh to be attempting the delineation of a character against a set of incongruous and unsuitable circumstances proving unbearable to him. The art of Waugh's comedy lies here in the comic presentation of Scott King who finds himself at sea in the vicious circle of politicians at Neutralia fighting for the cause of Neutralia rather than singing in honour of Bellorius, the famous Latin poet. It is a short narrative speaking out clearly as to how vice pays a lip service to virtue in the modern age of moral degradation. Here the comments of Anthony Burgess are noteworthy:

> If Waugh is to be remembered as a comic novelist that implies no relegation to a secondary status, as though it were a meaner achievement to make people laugh than to make

them cry. He recognised his kinship with P.G. Wodehouse, but comedy with him was not merely entertainment, summer holiday stuff; it was a medium for the expression of ultimate truths, some of them very bitter.[13]

The Loved One—An Anglo-American Tragedy, written during 1948, draws a ludicrous portrait of an unknown race of poor whites—called the Caucasians living by curious beliefs about life and death. Waugh had come across them at Hollywood on the edge of the great Californian desert. He had wondered at their curious worship of death being in their eyes the real liberator of man from his earthly sufferings. It was thus their cult for death that stirred his creative imagination and motivated him to write an Anglo-American tragedy with the help of characters like Joyboy Aimee and Dennis Barlowe, the mortician, the cosmetician and the British poet, respectively working in the Hollywood film industry in the fictional presentation of the *Loved One*, the novel. It deals with the love intrigue of Joyboy and Aimee who fall in love with each other but it is Dennis Barlowe also who takes a keen interest in wooing her by writing love-songs in praise of her beauty and comeliness. The Hollywood film industry is ringing with his romantic songs and lyrics. Aimee cannot make up her mind in the choice of her lover between Barlowe and Joyboy. Finding herself thus mentally perturbed in the matter of her final selection between the two lovers she writes a letter to Guru Brahmin, a Mr. Slump to give her advice on this matter, taking him as a wise counsellor of this issue of love-intrigue. To her utter surprise she gets the advice of committing suicide from him in view of her triangular love-intrigue which she really does also ruining her precious life thus on the one hand and leaving Joyboy forlorn and making Dannis Barlowe resign and become a non-sectarian clergyman on the other. The novel thus closes on a note of surprising satisfaction.

It is the weaving of plot and the delineation of character that draw one's attention here in the creation of this mock-heroic romance. The novel is sardonic in tone and serio-comic in theme. Waugh seems to be at a sublime height of success in the creation of such a splendid fiction of love-intrigue that provokes thought and laughter simultaneously. It, however, draws a successful portrait (in allegerical terms) of our modern civilization that makes one death-conscious owing to the very set-up of life having grown tragic and death-like. The curious beliefs of the Caucasians that love for death is the only cult of today and that committing suicide is no sin on this ground makes him paint in ghastly terms the picture of cemetery in keeping with the seriousness of his theme. The novel is as such a tragedy of the modern civilization itself which is full of such people as are having no roots of their own either in their soil or culture. Bereft of these strong forces they seem to be doomed to sterility like the Caucasians. *The Loved One* is, on this ground, in the words of Frederick J. Stopp, a satire; it is also, in its chosen allegorical mode, a work of great poetic tract and sensibility.[14]

Finally, we turn to Helena, a historical novel of Evelyn Waugh, dealing with the questioning religious spirit of the modern times. It draws the portrait of Emperor Helena who has a desire in her heart to search for a true cross to establish the historical reality of Christianity. She asks the Pope Sylvester to explain the riddle but the latter fails to satisfy her.

Helena explains the balsphemy of religion in the eyes of modern man who pays only a lip service to it instead of being actuated by a sense of devotion to it. It illustrates in the finest possible terms the struggle of the modern man between faith and doubt in the veracity of Christian Religion.

Helena, whatever the theme of this novel be, marks the conclusion of the middle phase of Waugh's career, and also proves the glorious triumph of Waugh as a writer of fiction. Yet, curiously enough, the end of this middle phase also signifies the beginning of a more brilliant and prosperous career awaiting him in the near future. It is not an exaggeration to point out the symptoms of his further growth of sentiment and sensibility. Like Fielding, Waugh also seems to be feeling by now that "life everywhere furnishes an accurate observer with the ridiculous." The following comments on Fielding made by Richard Church appear to be a fit commentary on Waugh as well:

> It is that spirit of all prevading charity, expressing itself in a genial but vigorous compassion which enabled Fielding to

bring to the novel for the first time, a completely dispassionate observing mind. The result was the appearance in fiction of real human beings, in light and shadow, in weakness and strength, action and thinking and feeling as you and I all other flesh and blood mortals behave during our lifelong conflict with the spirit that inhabits us. We are sinners, we are saints; and usually we are a neutral emulsion of the two. So are Tom Jones, and his lady Sophia, and Squire Allsworthy, and the rest of them, people who have commanded the interest of millions of readers, and the professional praise, through imitation, of all those hosts of writers who have come after him. Scott, Hazlitt, Lamb, Maria, Edgeworth, Jane Austom, Dickens and Thackeray, George Eliot and Meredith; these are a few of the great figures in literature who are his debtors.[15]

NOTES

1. Nancy Hale, *The Realities of Fiction*, London, Macmillan & Co. 1963, p. 48.
2. *Work Suspended*, Evelyn Waugh. Penguin Series, 1963, p. 112.
3. *Evelyn Waugh* by M. Bradbury, Edinburgh and London, 1964, p. 80.
4. Stopp, *The Portrait of an Artist*, p. 101.
5. *Put Out More Flags*. Evelyn Waugh, Penguin Series, 1966, p. 8.
6. *Ibid.*, p. 208.
7. *Ibid.*
8. *Ibid.*
9. Frederick J. Stopp, Evelyn Waugh. *The Portrait of an Artist*, p. 132.
10. *Roman Holiday*, A.A. De Vitis, 1958, Vision Press, p. 52.
11. *Brideshead Revisited*, Evelyn Waugh, Penguin Series, 1968, p. 246.
12. *The Dark Comedy*, T.L. Styan, Cambridge at the University Press, 1968, p. 39.
13. *The Spectator*, April, 15, 1966, p. 462.
14. Frederick J. Stopp, *The Portrait of an Artist*, p. 151.
15. *The Growth of the English Novel*, Richard Church, p. 79.

7
CHAPTER

The Final Phase of Evelyn Waugh's Writing Career (1952-61)

By the time one reaches the final phase of Evelyn Waugh's career as a novelist, one finds him at the plenitude of his artistic development. The middle phase of his career itself seems to have given a foretaste of the cultivation of the three-dimensional growth of his fiction, which is manifestly perfected at his hands in this period. His keen interest in the affairs of men and women, seen in a comic perspective, gives an earthly touch to his sentiment and sensibility. The outward and inward portrait of characters becomes his primary concern by this time, and this lends a note of versimilitude to his fiction. What is more, his very attitude to life has become serio-comic justifying thus the proverbial statement that life is a comedy and tragedy both at the same time. At this stage of his artistic career we are perhaps in a position to say in so many words by way of a conclusion about Evelyn Waugh as principally a writer of the novel of character. He is a writer taking his cue from the great tradition of English novelists like Henry Fielding, Jane Austen, George Eliot and Charles Dickens in whose novels characters stand out. Waugh seems to have been considerably impressed by the technique of their writing the full evidence of which we get at this final stage of his career. Somerset Maugham marks the value of characterisation in the following way which indirectly speaking seems to be the impression of Evelyn Waugh too. Maugham holds:

> At present there is a tendency to dwell on characterisation rather than on incident and of course, characterisation is important; for unless you come to know intimately the persons of a novel, and so can sympathise with them, you are unlikely to care what happens to them.[1]

Waugh too seems to be holding almost the same view when he says:

> "My problem has been to distill comedy and sometimes tragedy from the knockabout farce of peoples' outward behaviour."[2] The stress here is definitely on characterisation. The most important work of this period is *Sword of Honour* popularly known as the war trilogy. In addition to this there are other works like Love Among the Ruins and The Ordeal of Gilbert Pinfold which may be termed as the swan songs of Evelyn Waugh. The war trilogy entitled as *Sword of Honour*, consists of *Men at Arms*, *Officers and Gentlemen* and *Unconditional Surrender*—three novels projecting mainly the character of Guy Cronchback against the expansive background of the Second World War. At the same time all the three novels form one single unit on account of being a concentrated and continued study of Guy's military life.

Men at Arms, the first volume in the war trilogy narrates the story of Guy Crouchback, the youngest member of an old Catholic family. At the time of the outbreak of the Second World War he is staying alone in Italy. He is in constant touch with the newspaper which gives him full details about the war and also the position of his own country, England. Inspired by a true feeling of patriotism, he joins the Royal Corps of Halberdiers as a soldier under training. In course of his apprenticeship as a soldier he happens to come across Apthorpe, the eccentric temporary officer, Ritchie Hook the famous brigadier, De Souza the cynic, Trimmer a hairdresser, and many such trainees as are noted for their eccentricity and variety of tastes. In course of his sails on the Dekar expedition, as ill luck world have it, he indulges himself in an escapade arranged by the brigadier Ritchic Hook, which results in the death of Apthorpe. The fact is, he makes an injudicious gift of a bottle of whisky to Apthorpe while the latter is down with fever. As a consequence of this inglorious act, Guy is demoted and expelled out of the army.

Men at Arms is thus a minute and concentrated study of Guy Crouchback who in the first phase of his military career faces a sad consequence of his innocence. Written in a mock-heroic vein, the novel draws a faithful portrait of an innocent soldier who meets with an ignominious end owing to his complete ignorance of the vicious people passing their lives in the military field. His innocence of this kind makes one pity him. This is all the more so when we come to know about his wife Virginia Troy having divorced him. Incidentally, this woman is made to apepar as a flirt one who could by no means claim the creator's compassion. In *Men at Arms*, there seems to be a determined attempt on the part of Waugh to draw portraits of his characters in a most convincing and faithful way. Besides, Waugh is mocking here at the glorious tradition of military life which does not fit in at all with the unscrupulous character of the modern generation. He seems to be making a fun of the noble family Guy does belong to and describe quite clearly as to how badly it is facing crisis in the emergence of the common class of people having little sense of tradition. It often appears as if Waugh were making Guy the touchstone of his moral judgement on the odious character of the modern age in arms. The effect of the Russo-German alliance reflected in the following passage, enables us to make a convincing study of Guy's character in the wake of the modern age in arms:

> Just seven days earlier he had opened his morning newspaper on the headlines announcing the Russo-German Alliances. News that shook the politicians and young poets of a dozen capital cities brought deep peace to one English heart. Eight years of shame and loneliness were ended.... He expected his country to go to war in a panic, for the wrong reasons or for no reason at all, with the wrong allies, in pitiful weakness. But now, splendidly everything had become clear. The enemy at least was plain in view, huge and hateful, all disquise cast off. It was the Modern Age in Arms. Whatever the outcome there was a place for him in that battle.[3]

What draws our attention in the aforesaid passage is Guy's reaction to the shifting alliances of the world politics rather than the event of worldwide importance in the modern war. It is, as would often appear, the character of the modern age in arms rather than the character of an individual, be it Guy or anyone else that becomes an interesting and thought-provoking theme of study in the novel. The art of characterisation is as such born out of the situations and circumstances of the modern age. Most surprisingly, it is the character of the age that determines the plot of this novel or vice versa. The novel seems to have been written from the standpoint of the novelist's omniscience which naturally makes Waugh concentrate on a single character. This surely stands the novelist in good stead, thus leading him to excel in the art of characterisation. Somerset Maugham extols the value of a single character in the following words:

> The facts that the reader should know are imparted to him as the person through whom the story is told gradually learns them; and so the reader enjoys the pleasure of the elucidation, step by step, of what was puzzling, obscure and uncertain. The method thus gives the novel something of the mystery of detective story, and so that dramatic quality which Henry James was always eager to obtain.[4]

Men at Arms, observed in view of the aforesaid passage, achieves verisimilitude in full proportion. Also it is the military organisation which is the butt of Waugh's satiric art. Frederick J. Stopp calls the novel 'a comic war-novel' which might at a casual glance appear to be a paradox, but judged in the light of his own words, the whole thing would sound fully convincing:

> A comic war-novel is something of a contradiction in terms. "The organised dispossession, capture and killing of his own species" may be, in Mr. Waugh's own words, "among the activities which, like husbandry distinguish civilized man from brute creation". But the killing can only be heroic, grim, tragic, or senseless; it is the organisation which has its comedy. "Army life, with its humour, surprises and loyalties...comprises the very essence of human intercourse", Mr. Waugh continues in the same essay. So *Men at Arms* is a comic novel of army life, rather than of war.[5]

On the whole the novel ends as a brilliant comic achievement at the hands of Evelyn Waugh but the meat of the book, says Christopher Hollis, "is the study of the character of Guy Crouchback". In other words, this novel marks a complete triumph of the art of characterisation—a distinct advance in Waugh's fictional art.

Officers and Gentlemen the second volume of the war trilogy is again a concentrated study of Guy's character. This novel presents the portrait of Guy at a time he had attached himself again to command unit in the Hebridean Isle of Mugg. The Hebridean Isle of Mugg is a chosen place of the military camp where whisky flows freely and the omnipotent Laird receives deferential respect from H.M. Forces. Time is passing happily but there comes a moment of bitterness in this high comedy of Mugg when he meets with a military debacle in Crete at the hands of his enemies. As a result of this defeat he makes a total surrender to his enemies. It is, however, Trimmer, the hairdresser who is known as captain Mc Tavish also, surpasses him in earning a good name as a competent soldier by a ludicrous raid on the coast of occupied France. By virtue of this mock-heroic raid he wins the title of a national hero. His ludicrous victory is recorded in the glowing words of the General Whale:

> Captain Mc Tavish trained and led a small raiding force which landed on the coast of occupied France. On landing he showed a complete disregard of personal safety which communicated itself to his men...captain Mc Tavish, in spite of having sustained injuries in the course of the action, successfully re-embarked his whole force, without casualties, in accordance with the time-table. Throughout the latter phases of the operation he showed exemplary cooliness.[6]

Officers and Gentlemen thus seems to be a pointed and concentrated attack on the hollowness of a modern soldier who fights, only in name rather than in a spirit of chivalry. The character of Mc Tavish is portrayed in a spirit of levity intentionally to maintain the triviality of the theme in view of the meaninglessness of modern man's pursuit. To quote Frederick J. Stopp:

In presenting the character of Mc Tavish, the hairdresser getting an edge over Guy by achieving the title of the national hero on account of a ludicrous raid on the coast of the occupied France on the one hand and cuckolding him (Guy) on the other by having fallen in love with his wife, Virginia, Waugh seems to be writing in a mock-heroic vein creating comic situation and characters.[7]

Admittedly, this novel exposes the meaninglessness and futility of the modern age-in-arms. It shows the travesty of modern civilization as a whole which seems to be based on the foundation of lies and political chicanery. This amounts to a confirmation of the fact that vice has to pay only a lip service to virtue these days. So, Hollis comments:

> *Officers and Gentlemen* ends with Guy's depression on learning of the Nazi invasion of Russia. While others around welcome this on purely opportunist grounds, to Guy it means the end of any possibility of finding meaning in the war with evil, as is now the case, embattled upon both sides.[8]

Officers and Gentlemen thus deals in the finest possible manner with the absurdities of the modern age in arms. The sarcastic presentation of Trimmer, pitchforked into the status of a national hero in contrary to the pious and innocent character of Guy as a soldier of conventional morality reduces the military glory to its non-entity. Waugh's satiric art as such seems to be doubly benefitted from the point of view of mock heroic presentation, deriding on the one hand the conventional code of Military life and on the other the modern age in arms based on a foundation of deciet and guerrilla tacties. It is as such a further study of Guy's disillusionment, the evidence of which is found in clear-cut terms in his stiff reaction to the consequences of the war noted below:

> It was just such a sunny, breezy Mediterranean day two years before when he read of the Russo-German alliance, when a decade of shame seemed to be ending in light and reason, when the Enemy was plain in view, huge and hateful, all disguise cast off; the modern age in arms.

> Now that hallucination was dissolved like the whales and turtles on the voyage from Crete, and he was back after less than two years' pilgrimage in a Holy Land of illusion in the old ambiguous world, where priests were spies and gallant friends proved traitors and his country was led blundering into dishonour.[9]

It is as a veteran cartoonist that Waugh appears here in this novel painting the varied shades of Guy's character vis-à-vis Trimmer's whose figure is in the words of Frederick J. Stopp "the figure of the people in arms, a development of Hooper in *Brideshead Revisited*". Not merely that, "he is the new and ugly reality", adds Frederick J. Stopp again, "which supplements the old illusion which was Apthorpe; he is the denial of all form, tradition, honour. A fraud himself, he is quick to recognise the fraud in others, in head-waiters for instance with their phoney French; he is, free of the underworld of the spurious, and succeeds, at a long remove Guy and Tommy Black house in the favours of Virginia. His very metamorphoses, from Trimmer the Cockney to Gustave the hairdresser, then to Mc the Major of Argylls, parody the varied roles of a Grimes or a Philbrick, and the spasmic changes of military life...." Heroes are in strong demand, but not such a Guy, the 'upper class' and the 'Fine flower of the Nation'. This is a People's War, says I N Kilbannock, "with cynical flare of the publicity man." We want heroes of the people, to or for the people, by, with and from the people. In short they want Trimmer....[10]

Officers and Gentlemen thus records Guy Crouchleack's military career coming to an unhappy climax with the defeat and withdrawal from Crete that had begun so spiritedly in *Men at Arms*. *Unconditional Surrender* (1961) completes the war trilogy of Evelyn Waugh. If tells the story of Guy's reconciliation with Virginia Troy, his wife who had deserted him. It is she who takes the initiative for this reconciliation as she having come in the family way in liaision with Trimmer who declines to help her in getting an abortion, feels pressed under such circumstances to take her last refuge in Guy. She becomes a Catholic at his instance getting an absolution from her past sins before a priest and baptises her child as 'little Trimmer' as a Catholic. Guy accepts the child after that as a Catholic heir to his family on the ground of all differences being theological only in nature and is guided by his father's letter before his death conveying the message:

> Quantitative judgements don't apply. If only one soul was saved, that is full compensation for any amount of 'loss of face'. Virginia dies afterwards leaving little Trimmer behind her being severely hit by a bomb along with Peregrine, Guy's uncle. The little Trimmer is then brought up by Guy later on.

Unconditional Surrender gives an introspective report of a man who is not in a mood to surrender himself to the challenging forces of modern generation in spite of his feelings having been injured by them. He has taken his last refuge in Catholicism in view of an almost total disintegration of social, political, moral and intellectual values all around. He seems to have made a final discovery of his self and taken the ultimate decision to embrace the Catholic Church. To quote Christopher Hollis:

> He finds himself everywhere in the company of people with no roots, no understanding of what life is about, no sense of the dignity of its purpose. They have adopted left-wing opinions since such opinions are now in fashion and to the advantage of one's career. Adopting such opinions, they have surrendered to a total callousness to the appalling barbarities that are being committed in the name of these principles.... It leaves us with a picture of the world in which one institution alone—the Catholic Church—remains in protest against the nihilistic pointlessness of the modern age and of course the Catholic church in the world of Crouchback utters its protest in accents somewhat different from those that have been employed by some spokesman of the church in this new age of aggiornamento. It is a church in protest against the age, not a church that seeks in any way to accommodate itself to the age.[11]

The novel bears a clear-cut evidence of Waugh's maturity and proficiency in character-painting. The portrait of Peregrime, Guy's uncle, is drawn sarcastically by him in the following way which often speaks of a master-craftsman:

> He is a "man of many interests certainly well read, widely travelled, minutely informed in many recondite subjects, a discovering collector of bibelots; a man handsomely apparelled and adorned when he did duty at the papal court; a man nevertheless assiduously avoided even by those who shared his interests. He exemplified the indefinable numbness which Guy recognised intermittently in himself; the saturnine strain.... He was naturally frugal and welcomed the excuse to forgo wine and food, to wear his old clothes and to change his linen weekly. He was quite without fear for his own safety when the bombs were falling. He rejoiced to see many of his gloomier predictions of foreign policy fulfilled.[12]

The appropriate use of bathos in the character-portrayal of Peregrine carries out a sense of satiric touch to the passage giving a clear insight into Waugh's art of fiction-writing.

Sword of Honour, known thus as a war-trilogy, mirrors the thoughts and reflections of Waugh's reaction to the war and its aftermath. It is in the words of Bernard Bergonzi, "an episodic work certainly but it is big enough to accommodate a good deal of material which is rather casually linked together." Bernard Bergonzi goes on to say "Indeed, one of the most remarkable things about *Sword of Honour* is that, although written by an author of strongly right-wing views, it is one of the most thorough-going satires of military life on record. Guy's career in the army is totally inglorious, even if for no fault of his own. He is subjected to a remarkable variety of defeats and humiliations."[13] But the most candid and fearless observation is that of John St. John, who writes to say:

> Evelyn's novels are a splendid antidote to the glamorised, lying version of 1939-45 that is now the mode. They provide the truest as well as the funniest, guide to the war as I know it.[14]

Finally, it could well be noted that the episodical character of the Trilogy is not only convincing but is also adequately-redeemed by the consistent and determined concentration on characterisation. Plot and story-aspects that comprise varieties of incidents, indeed a curious medley of situations from the shockingly trivial to the movingly ennobbling—give way under the pressure of powerful characterisation. The trilogy, in other words, is by far, a milestone in Waugh's career as a novelist.

Love Among the Ruins

Love Among the Ruins: A Romance of the Near Future (1953), is an attempt on the part of Evelyn Waugh to portray the world of the near future in view of the social, political and moral crises of today. It tells the story of Miles Plastic, a young man who is convicted for arson and sent to Mountjoy, a rehabilitation centre for his treatment. He is pronounced cured after some time and sent to work in the State Euthanasia centre where he happens to fall in love with Clara, a ballet-dancer. She comes in the family way in liaison with him and the would-be baby is ruined in the womb due to the injurious effect of a sterilization operation on her. The most surprising effect of the operation is that due to the operation having gone wrong, she develops a handsome beard. Miles Plastic, unable to bear this incalculable grief, burns down the Mountjoy castle out of frustration.

This short novel, written in a serio-comic-vein, is a sad and gloomy presentation of the terrible future awaiting mankind. Manifestly a novel of imagination, it seems to have been written in the satiric vein of Aldous Huxley's *The Brave New World* and George Orwell's photographic novel of the future 1984. While the humour is borne out, in the presentation of a handsome beard over Clara's face due to the operation having gone wrong, a note of sadness is revealed in the death of the baby in the womb itself.

Significantly, Evelyn Waugh does not spare even the Welfare State which introduces Euthanasia as a modern device to reform one's criminal behaviour. He attacks the policy of the Euthanasia Centre in a comic vein:

> Euthanasia had not been part of the original 1945 Health Service, it was a Tory measure designed to attract votes from the aged and the mortally sick. Under the Bevan-Eden Coalition the Service came into general use and won

> instant popularity. The Union of Teachers was pressing for its application to different children. Foreigners came in such numbers to take advantage of the service that immigration authorities now turned back the bearers of single tickets.[15]

It is on these grounds that Frederick J. Stopp holds:

> Mr. Waugh's story never loses its astringent humour, freedom from sentiment. Both qualities are guaranteed, not only by his own style and out-book, but also in this particular case by the beard.[16]

Indeed, this successful fusion of pathos and humour achieved by Waugh in the slight story under consideration should put him comfortably beside one of the greatest masters of this craft-Sterne. The reference is to the latter's masterpiece, Tristram Shandy.

The Ordeal of Gilbert Pinfold (1957)

The Ordeal of Gilbert Pinfold is the psychoanalytical study of a middle-aged novelist who goes on a voyage to Ceylone as per the advice of his doctor to change his climate due to his frequent illness. In course of his voyage in the ship he comes across a band of existentialists of psychoanalysts who with the help of their box measure the life forces of an individual. Their actions on board the ship make him feel suspicious of their intentions. He feels as if they were having some ulterior motive behind the use of their box. His inner voices suggest different reactions of his heart to their behaviour, as a result of which he finds himself in an embarrassing position. Under the influence of a wrong kind of drug consumed by him, he has got a hallucination of having come in the clutch of some people whose main motive is to kill him. He complains of this murderous intention to Steerforth, the captain of the ship, but he does not find any such thing going to happen on board the ship, on making inquiry. Pinfold then feels suspicious of the intentions of Steerforth himself taking him too for a murderer. He gets nervous and writes in a fit of emotion a letter to his wife informing her in full details about the actions of these B.B.C. people who as he writes to his wife "have made themselves a great nuisance to me on board. They have got a lot of apparatus with them, most of it new and experimental".

Not only that, he further writes in the same letter, "They are trying to psychoanalyse me. I know this sounds absurd. The Germans at the end of the war were developing this Box for the examination of prisoners. The Russians have perfected it.... As you can imagine it's hellish invention in the wrong hands."

Getting this letter Mrs. Pinfold gets mentally disturbed and advises him in her reply to come back soon. She rather manages to send some one to take him back to Lychpole but in the meantime, Mr. Pinfold himself is back safe and sound having come unhurt and victorious out of the ordeal he seems to have faced on board the ship. Dr. Drake, his family physician re-examines him finding these symptoms to have been the effect of the pills on him administered by him.

This is what the story is all about in a nutshell, but the novel termed as 'a conversation-piece' by Waugh himself studies the character of Gilbert Pinfold in a most pyscho-analytical manner. It is a concentrated study of a mind, torn and bruised by the abnormal forces of the outside world. He is a middle-aged author keeping himself confined within his cloistered shell of imagination. His tastes and attitudes are as such not at all in keeping with those of his age as it is clearly illustrated in the following passage:

> His strongest tastes were negative. He abhorred plastics, Picasso, sunbathing, and jazz—everything in fact that had happened in his own lifetime. The tiny kindling of charity which came to him through his religion sufficed only to temper his disgust and change it to beredom.[17]

Waugh seems to be at his best while portraying the character of Gilbert Pinfold in the above passage. It is the portrait of an individual who finds himself to be a total misfit in the company of strangers in the outside world. Pinfold thus appears to be a schizophrenic character suffering from hallucinations having their origin in his inward mind. He is an abnormal individual in whose opinion the whole world is a place of rogues and charlatans. Whomsoever he meets in his day-to-day life, they seem to him to be full of deceit and humbug, evil intentions. He is the picture of a novelist keeping himself aloof from the up-to-date progress of the world and judges his age in terms of his own abnormal values and attitudes. On such grounds he seems to be either a genius 'whose wits are sure to madness near allied' or a bore of the first grade in view of his impressions, attitudes and predilections. As a novelist he is conventional in his themes and techniques which Waugh clarifies below:

> The basic qualities of a Pinfold novel seldom vary and may be enumerated thus: Conventionality of plot, falseness of characterisation, morbid sentimentality, gross and Backneyed farce alternating with grosser and more hackneyed melodrama; cloying religiosity, which will be found tedious or blesphemous according as the reader shares or repudiates his doctrinal preconceptions, an adventitious and offensive sensuality that is clearly introduced for commercial motives. All this is presented in a style which, when it varies from the trite, lapses into positive illiteracy.[18]

This novel, presented as a conversation-piece, appears to be an admirable attempt on the part of Evelyn Waugh to portray a psycho-analytical picture of character and certifies the splendid success of the author in the art of characterisation. One could easily witness the reflections of Pinfold's mind in his reactions to the outward world. Moreover, the novel bears the mark of the stream-of-consciousness technique of Virginia Woolf too, particularly in the intense study of the inner world, the world of the mind.

Yet, what gives this novel its essential flavour is its autobiographical character. To quote Hollis:

> *Confessedly* almost autobiographical it is the account of a voyage taken to Ceylone by a successful middle-aged novelist who is ill because he has consumed the wrong sort of sleeping draught. He is assailed by voices which threaten him and make obscene suggestions to him. The book opens with a chapter of ruthlessly searching autobiographical analysis, in the form of an analysis of the character of Gilbert Pinfold, and many readers have found these the most interesting chapters in the book. Some have professed to find the chapters of near-madness amusing.[19]

The novel raises a very important question as to why Pinfold acts in an abnormal way. Mr. Priestley is reported to have asked the same question in the New Statesman (31 August 1957) "What was wrong with Mr. Pinfold?" Incidentally, it is Mr. Frederick J. Stopp who gives a satisfactory answer:

> The answer is—apart from the false medication which was the physical cause of the voices-nothing. To assume that anything was wrong with Mr. Pinfold is rather like assuming that a satirist is just a man with a grievance. A satirist is a man with an infinite possibility of creative irritation when observing the behaviour of his fellow-men; Mr. Pinfold was in the same fruitful state when observing the behaviour of his own inner mind. The point of Mr. Priestly's article was that Mr. Waugh should give up the pretence of living the life of the Catholic country-gentleman, and settle down to being a writer; this was the recipe which would banish boredom, drink, and strain. People have been saying this to Mr. Waugh for twenty years.[20]

The novel on the whole is a tour-de-force at the hands of the master craftsman, Evelyn Waugh.

This novel is not just a document of grievances, coming from any angry observer. That would have reduced it to a kind of a manifesto. But Waugh is too much of an artist (and a conscious artist at that) to subordinate art to satire. In fact, the novel is a demonstration of the very reverse; it is satire that has been successfully subordinated to art—the art of novel-writing. What is more, one salutes in the author of this novel a mature artist, who is definitely at the highest point of his achievement.

NOTES

1. Ten Novels and their Authors, Somerset, p. 23.
2. E. Waugh.
3. *Men at Arms*, p. 12.
4. (The Art of Fiction) Ten Novels and Their Authors. Somerset Mangham Penguin Book, 1969, pp. 14-15.
5. Evelyn Waugh, *Portrait of an Artist*, Federick J. Stopp, p. 158.
6. *Officers and Gentlemen*, p. 150.

7. Evelyn Waugh, *Portrait of an Artist,* Frederick J. Stopp, p. 170.
8. Evelyn Waugh, Christopher Hollis, p. 34.
9. *Officers and Gentlemen*, p. 240.
10. F.J. Stopp, *Evelyn: Portrait of an Artist.* London, Chapman Hall Ltd., 27 Essex Street WC. 2, p. 170.
11. Evelyn Waugh, Christopher Hollis, Published (1971) for the British Council by Longman Group Ltd., p. 35.
12. *Unconditional Surrender*, E. Waugh, p. 124.
13. *The Listener*, Feb. 20, 1964, p. 306.
14. *Sunday Times*, Sept. 7, 1969 "Temporary *Officers and Gentlemen.*" John St. John, p. 10.
15. *Love Among the Ruins*. Penguin Series, 1962, p. 194.
16. Frederick J. Stopp, *Evelyn Waugh: Portrait of an Artist*, p. 157.
17. *The Ordeal of Gilbert Pinfold*, Penguin Series, 1962, p. 14.
18. *Ibid.*, p. 62.
19. *Evelyn Waugh*, Christopher Hollis, p. 38.
20. E. Waugh, *Portrait of an Artist*, Frederick J. Stopp, p. 232.

8 CHAPTER Evelyn Waugh's Points of View

Like other writers of his time, Evelyn Waugh too has his own points of view without knowing which a fairly correct estimate of his mind and art might become difficult to get. He writes his works from different angles of view which may comprise his ulterior approaches to life—social, political, moral, intellectual and philosophical. It is true that his artistic point of view is hardly to be understimated in this context, but the way he chooses life to see seems to be assuming a greater significance than any other point of view.

However, it is always risky to commit in this respect about the points of view incorporated in his works of art, but a mere guesswork and a bit of scrutiny into his artistic leanings should make one aware of his social, political, moral and intellectual points of view. As a social satirist, Waugh seems to be delineating the common follies and foibles of a developing society of today which are clearly reflected in his earlier works, namely *Decline and Fall*, *Vile Bodies*, *Black Mischief*, *A Handful of Dust* and others. A careful study of these works explains the threads of meaning interwoven with one another in a harmonious fashion. *Decline and Fall*, for instance, is a study of the modern trends of society in view of the scientific and intellectual advancement of human being. The character of Paul Pennybeather, seen in this light, seems to have been delineated ironically in the wake of the decline and fall of old social values. Paul is a misfit in the present society due to his oversimplicity and utter ignorance of the inherent tricks of a sophisticated milieu. Waugh's mind in this first novel thus seems to be absorbed in a minute study of the social milieu of his time. The point of view, as such, from which the novel seems to have been written is social as well as intellectual. The decision of the Domestic Bursar and the Junior Dean to make Paul Pennyfeather quit the college because "That sort of young man does the college no good"[1] strikes violently at the very edifice of the university education that has gone meaningless and farce. As a writer of social comedy, Waugh seems to have made his first experiment in this novel the later growth of which finds its evidence in his *Vile Bodies*, *Black Mischief*, and *A Handful of Dust*. All these novels, taken together, represent the moral and intellectual crises of the transition period Waugh belonged to. Waugh's attitudes to art and society seem to have been clearly reflected in his further studies of the dying culture of modern age. *Vile Bodies*, his second novel strikes at the very malaise of human society that seems to be seriously suffering from the mushroom growth of parties stated in a parenthesis in the following way:

> Oh, Nina, what a lot of parties; (...Masked parties, Savage parties, Victorian parties, Greek parties, Wild West parties, Russian parties, Circus parties, parties where one had to dress as somebody else, almost naked parties, in St. John's Wood, parties in flats and studios and houses and ships and hotels and night clubs; in windmills and swimming baths, tea parties at school where one ate muffins and meringues and tinned crab, parties at Oxford where one drank brown sherry and smoked Turkish cigarettes, dull dances in London and comic dances in Scotland and disgusting dances in Paris—all the succession and repetition of massed humanity.... These vile bodies...).[2]

The above passage illustrates the moral crisis of the present civilization that feeds on a number of irrational pursuits represented by various sorts of parties mentioned here. It seems as if Waugh were writing as an existentialist diving deep into the innermost recesses of human society. His approaches to society are as such seldom one and the same. He treats his social and political themes from the points of view of an existentialist, a social reformer, a humanist reflecting on the decline and fall as well as the progress of man's civilization. It is true that in treating his interesting themes he might be appearing in various colours, but one easily marks the avoidance of comments on his part that keeps his personality disguised to us. Whatever the points of view underlying his early works of art, his aims are non-commital. To quote Frederick J. Stopp:

> The critic who seeks to display the inner mechanism of this world may well be seized with trepidation. Not only does the author refuse to be drawn by those who seek 'to detect cosmic significance in his work', 'to relate it to fashions in philosophy, social predicaments or psychological tensions.' His self-confessed positive aims are just as non-committal. They may be reduced to two; he writes to delight an audience, and he produces books as would a craftsman.[3]

By looking into the moral implications of a Waugh novel, one could thus easily mark the impartial gesture he seems to be maintaining at the time of writing. Frederick J. Stopp clearly and succinctly illustrates the fear of relating the significance of these novels to 'fashions in philosophy, social predicaments or psychological tensions' in case the inner implications of his novels are sought by us but he seems to be warning us of the risks too in making such an attempt on account of Waugh's attitude of the avoidance of comment on his part. It is on account of such an attitude on his part that Frederick J. Stopp makes his further comments in the following words:

> His silence, in his own person, on his own intentions, is parallelled by his avoidance of comment, as narrator, or the processes in the mind of the creatures. There is an almost complete absence of introspective analysis and of that ironic comment so much affected by writers of our century. Take for instance, the opening sentences of *A Handful of Dust*: "Was anyone hurt?... No one, I am thankful to say," said Mrs. Beaver, "except two housemaids who lost their heads and jumped through a glass roof into the paved court."[4]

It is clear then that Waugh's novels contain different strands of meaning no doubt, though Waugh seldom feels like making any commitment insofar as his points of view in his novels are concerned. Even in his famous work *A Handful of Dust* Waugh in spite of apparently seeming to attack the very outward progress of humanity keeps his intentions concealed from us. It is no doubt true that the novel presents a minute study of a disintegrated family due to the sudden break in conjugal ties, but he does not declare his intentions and attitudes in so many words. Waugh maintains the following point of view only with regard to this novel:

> *A Handful of Dust*...dealt entirely with behaviours. It was humanist and contained all I had to say about humanism.[5]

Waugh's hints mentioned above fail to explain his intentions in clear-cut terms; they simply arouse one's curiosity rather than satisfy it. The novel seems to have been however written from the psychological point of view because of Waugh's preoccupation with the mental recesses of his characters like Tony Last and Brenda. The theme of the novel is definitely speaking a minute study of the disintegration of a family life due to the clash in conjugal ties not motivated by any selfishness but by the very boredom and ennui of the rural surrounding. This point of view is clearly substantiated even by Walter Allen in a short but subtle analysis of Waugh's novels in his famous critical book *Tradition and Dream*:

> It is a story of the destruction of Tony Last by his wife Brenda, a destruction motivated not by malignance, indeed scarcely motivated at all, but the outcome of boredom and irresponsible selfishness.[6]

Waugh's creative mind seems to have studied the human behaviour from varied angles of view enabling his reader thus to have a comprehensive insight into the riddles of human life. Every work of art created by him appears to be as such an experiment in itself, enabling his readers to have a vivid peep into the functioning of his brain. The more one proceeds in the exploration of his mind and art, the greater the number of nuances of human life is perceived by him. It is not only the social theme that engage his attention, but the political and moral theme as well which seems to have automatically emerged out of the social implication discussed by him. In *Put Out More*

Flags, his interests and attitudes to life appear to have widened considerably. Written during the time of the Great Bore War, the novel appears to be topical in nature dealing with the tides of international politics. The novel as such seems to have been written from the political social and moral points of view getting their reflection in the behaviour of his characters in the world of his fiction. One could get the confirmation of this view in his own statement made in his letter addressed to Mr. Churchill when he writes:

> I find more food for thought in the follies of Basil Seal and Ambrose Silk, than in the sagacity of the higher command. These characters are no longer contemporary in sympathy; they were forgotten even before the war; but they lived on delightfully in holes and corners and, like everyone else, they have been disturbed in their habits by the rough intrusion of current history.[7]

Brideshead Revisited bears the sign of Waugh's full maturity of mind, thus providing a successful study of all its dimensions. The theme here is decidedly eschatological which seems to have been written from the Catholic point of view. It is as a moralist that Waugh appears here to be questioning the validity of the material advancement of human life. It presents a profound study of a Catholic family facing a grave challenge of survival in the wake of the unreasonable growth of modern humanism. The conflict between science and religion is explicitly discussed in the study of his novel by Patricia Corr:

> What is significant from the Catholic point of view is that, however estranged one section of the family becomes from the other, however far the one strays from the Catholic roots, they have all one characteristic in common—an impressive conviction of the truth of their religion. "It is nonsense?" asks Sebastian of Charles, "I wish it were. It sometimes sounds terribly sensible to me." Julia, in reply to Charles's "...you do know at heart that 'its' all bosh, don't you?" says simply. How I wish it were. Behind the convictions of his characters is Mr. Waugh's own testimony of truth of the Catholic claims which may be temporarily ignored and

> rejected but not permanently denied. *Brideshead Revisited* succeeds in conveying the tremendous power of Catholicism in the lives of its adherents, a power which is due, not to mystical or superstitious forces, but to the shattering truth of its claims.[8]

It becomes thus abundantly clear how Evelyn Waugh interprets his points of view in a number of ways in his different kinds of work in accordance with the themes adopted by him therein. As a narrator he appears to be in link with his works in many ways providing thus a successful insight into the various implications of his artistic success. Waugh seems to have a sure grasp of the effects his works are meant to produce on the mind of his readers. His novels are in this sense a great achievement on his part from the point of view of art. Perhaps this led Percy Lubbock to comment on the critical value of the points of view in general in the following words:

> The whole intricate question of method, in the craft of fiction, I take to be governed by the question of the point of view the question of the relation in which the narrator stands to the story.[9]

Judged in the light of the above statement, Waugh as a narrator would seem to stand related in various ways to his works of art, often assuming the omniscient point of view and the impressionistic method of the first person. In the early phase of his artistic career he writes from the omniscient point of view. But in the middle phase of his career, he appears to have preferred the use of the first person in his narrative technique. He employs this freedom of choice deliberately with a view to creating a desirable effect on his readers. In this respect, his fiction seems to be a happy blending of various strands—omniscient, impressionistic, dramatic, oblique, partial and impartial. *Decline and Fall*, for instance, written from the omniscient point of view, does not fail to be oblique. The description of the Llanabba Castle as quoted below, is a sufficient evidence of this implication:

> Llanabba Castle presents two quite different aspects, according as you approach it from the Bangor or the Coast road. From the back it looks very much like any other large

country houses and the roofs of innumerable non-descript kitchen buildings, disappearing into the trees.[10]

But conversely the following description of the ways and means employed for the erection of this building is no less interesting when Waugh again writes just a few sentences further:

> The explanation of the rather striking contrast is simple enough. At the time of the cotton famine in the Sixties Llanabba house was the property of the prosperous Lancashire Millowner. His wife could not bear to think of their men starving; in fact, she and her daughters organised a little bazar in their aid, though without any very substantial results. Her husband had read the Liberal economists and could not think of paying without due return. Accordingly, 'enlightened self-interest' found a way. An encampment of mill-hand was settled in the park, and they were put to work walling the grounds and facing the house with great blocks of stone from a neighbouring quarry. At the end of the American war they returned to their mills, and Llanabba House became Llanabba castle after a great deal of work had been done very cheaply.[11]

The pictorial description of the Llanabba house turning into the Llanabba Castle is followed by the oblique point of view. Evelyn Waugh's point of view varies with the spirit of the description deserving appropriate treatments at appropriate places. As a writer of modern fiction, he maintains a wonderful equilibrium between the modern technique of fiction and conventional form of writing. By choosing the omniscient point of view he places himself in the category of the traditional school of novelists like Henry Fielding and Jane Austen on the one hand and puts himself in the line of Henry James, Somerset Maugham and the famous American novelist Herman Melville on the other by modifying the omniscient point of view a little to suit his genius and artistic device. Waugh uses this sort of omniscience on a single character, concentrating the camera of his imagination on the delineation of the varied aspects of his personality. The result of this modification in the omniscient point of view makes him able to put before his readers a thorough and convincing study of the nuances of his character. He here seems to have emulated the points of view of Somerset Maugham who discovers the sub-variety of this omniscient point of view. To quote Maugham:

> The novel written from the point of view of omniscience runs the risk of being unwieldy, verbal and diffuse. None has written it better than Tolstoy, but even he is not free from these imperfections.[12]

Maugham goes on to substantiate his argument thus:

> I suppose it was because Henry James with his solicitude for form in the novel became conscious of these disadvantages that he devised what may be described as a sub-variety of the method of omniscience. In this the author is still omniscient, but his omniscience is concentrated on a single character, and since the character is fallible the omniscience is not complete....
>
> The usefullness of the device, as Henry James without doubt very well saw, is that since this particular character in *The Ambassadors*, Strether, is all important, and it is through what he sees, hears, feels, thinks, surmises that the story is told and the characters of the other persons concerned in it are unfolded, the author finds it easy to resist the irrelevant. The construction of his novel is necessarily complete.[13]

Evelyn Waugh makes us (for instance) see and feel his reaction to the impact of the Second World War through the delineation of his famous character Guy Cronchback, a soldier living in the cloistered shell of his illusory world. As Strether is in *The Ambassadors* so are Paul Pennyfeather, Guy Cronchback, Adam Symes and Tony Last in the works of Evelyn Waugh. What is more, he has often employed the first person narrative to produce an everlasting effect on the minds of his readers by making his principal character comment from time to time like the chorus in a Greek tragedy. In employing such a technique Waugh seems to be emulating the style of Herman Melville as revealed in *Moby Dick*. *Brideshead Revisited* is an example where Waugh seems to have followed the technique of Herman Melville. To quote Maugham again for a full clarification of this point of view:

> Like the chorus in a Greek tragedy, he reflects on circumstances which he witnesses; he may lament, he may advise, he had no power to influence the course of events. He takes the reader into his confidence, tells him what he knows, hopes or fears, and when he is nonplussed frankly tells him so.... The narrator and the reader are united in their common interest in the persons of the story, their characters, motives and conduct; and narrator begets in the reader the same sort of familiarity with the creatures of his invention as he has himself.[14]

Judged in the light of the above statement, *Brideshead Revisited* would appear to be enormously successful. Waugh has demonstrated an unerring grasp of the points of view that has helped him most in realising his avowed aim as a modern novelist.

His fiction is thus an extended metaphor which is worthy to be termed as romance, allegory, satire and comedy. Noted below is an exhaustive account of the different strands of narrative usually found in modern fiction:

> The novel, dominated by its growing realistic conception of the individual in an actual society, neverthless has drawn upon mythic, historical and romantic patterns for its narrative articulation. The great historical narrative and the great allegorical romance also have combined many of the strands of narrative in their rich fabrics. Romance tends to didactic allegory or mimetic plotting or romantic adventure in order to captivate and move its audience. Myth mimesis, history, romance and fable all function so as to enhance one another and reward the narrative artist whose mind and art are so powerful that he can contain and control the richest combination of narrative possibilities.[15]

Obviously, what is striking here is the fact that the points made above would apply to Evelyn Waugh's art of fiction feeding on a cluster of impressions working in his mind. His points of view are as such never the same all the time in view of the comprehensive vision he seems to have adopted in the art of his fiction-writing.

NOTES

1. *Decline and Fall*, Evelyn Waugh. Penguin Series, 1968, p. 13. Made and Printed in Great Britain.
2. *Vile Bodies*, Evelyn Waugh, Penguin Series, 1967, p. 123.
3. Federick J. Stopp, pp. 181-82.
4. *Ibid.*
5. Evelyn Waugh, *Portrait of an Artist*, Frederick J. Stopp, p. 100.
6. *Tradition and Dream*. Walter Allen. Phoenix House, London, 1964, p. 210.
7. *Put Out More Flags*, Evelyn Waugh, p. 9.
8. Autumn 1962. The Spectator. Evelyn Waugh: Sanity and Catholicism Patricia Corr., p. 395.
9. The Craft of Fiction-Percy Lubbock-Jonathan Cape Thirty Bedford Square, London, 1960, p. 251.
10. *Decline and Fall*, p. 21.
11. *Ibid.*
12. Ten novels and their authors, W.S. Maugham. Penguin Book, 1969, pp. 14-15.
13. *Ibid.*
14. Ten novels and their authors, W.S. Maugham. Penguin Book, 1969. Made and Printed in Great Britain (Chaucer Press), p. 17.
15. "Plot in Narrative" by Robert Schools and Robert Kellogg in *Perspectives on Fiction*, Edited by James L. Calderwood and Harold E. Toliver, University of California, Irvine, New York Oxford University Press, London Toronto, 1968, p. 297.

9

CHAPTER

Conclusion

It is time some concrete points were made by way of a conclusion. First of all, it should be clear from whatever has been discussed about Waugh's mind and art that Waugh is the reviving link of the eighteenth century mode of fiction-writing with some pardonable modifications. It appears he has chosen ingeniously the old trend of fiction-writing introduced by Defoe, Richardson, Fielding, Smollett and Sterne and later, developed and refined by Jane Austen, Dickens, and George Eliot in the nineteenth century. Finding himself standing at the cross-roads of fiction-writing, the present novelist has very judiciously endeavoured to exploit the themes and conventions of his time in his best possible way catering to the tastes of the common mass of readers. His discerning intellect thus makes him choose the same style of writing which would sufficiently suit his creative imagination as well as the mind of common readers. From this point of view, Waugh seems to be writing fiction very much in tune with the spirit of his times. He seems to have established a happy blend of remanticism and realism in view of the tangled web of controversy over the art of fiction-writing generated by the master-builders of fiction like Virginia Woolf, D.H. Lawrence, James Joyce on the one hand and Aldous Huxley, C.P. Snow, Graham Greene on the other. Waugh appears to have arrived at this conclusion after much ado which might be termed a kind of compromise formula adopted by him to get through the wrangle of dispute amicably. On this score he would appear to be in unison with George Orwell whose ingenious use of this formula is by now an established fact. To take the names of some novels corroborating this strategy of fiction-writing, there are *Animal Farm* (1945) and *Nineteen Eighty-Four* (1949) written by Orwell and the *Loved One* (1948), and *Love Among the Ruins* (1953) written by Evelyn Waugh. They resemble in many ways with regard to their themes and their writers' attitudes to the time and their penchant for the romantic garb of writing. It is on account of this compromising attitude that David Lodge's following observation appears to be convincing:

> The situation of the novelist today may be compared to a man standing at a cross-roads. The road on which he stands (I am thinking primarily of the English novelist) is the realistic novel, the compromise between fictional and empirical modes. In the fiftees there was a strong feeling that this was the main road, the central tradition of English novel, coming down through the Victorians and Edwardians, temporarily diverted by modernist experimentalism but subsequently restored (by Orwell, Isherwood, Greene, Waugh, Powell, Angus Wilson, C.P. Snow, Amis, Sillitoe, Wain, etc. etc.) to its true course.[1]

In view of the observation mentioned above, the choice of a via media technique of treating a theme assumes a powerful importance in the eyes of these writers and Waugh as such does not appear as an exception to this general notion of the artists of this period. His achievement is distinguished by a careful maintenance of a happy equilibrium, a virtue that a comic writer would easily exploit to advantage. Very often the question of attaching a particular or specific kind of label to his writings arises in our mind, but perhaps nothing very categorical could be said of a writer whose value as an artist lies in concealing his art. Perhaps this may account for the bulk of tentative criticism of his novels a fact which has led to so much rethinking in the recent years. (The present dissertation itself is a case in point.) Waugh has revealed himself in the world of his novels to his readers in varied moods and colours but he leaves much upon them to explore his mind and art. To my mind he appears to be a great naturalist who without deceiving himself as well as his readers considers it to be his primary duty to present the illusion of reality in a matter of fact manner. Like Mona Lisa he invites the judgement of scholars and critics alike without reacting in any way to their remarks and attitudes to him. However, this could be said of him with a measure of certainty that he acts as an artist of the eighteenth century considering his principal task to deal with the follies and foibles of the society he lives in. He is as such in a close link with the great tradition of fiction-writing keeping the vision of the future too in the store of his creative imagination. He seems to be a writer of bi-focal imagination having a keen insight into the glorious tradition of the past and an acute awareness of the future in his dream. Thus he has got an acute historical sense which "compels a man to write" as T.S. Eliot remarks, "not merely with his own generation in his bones, but with a feeling that the whole of the literature of his own country has a simultaneous existence and composes a simultaneous order. This historical sense, to quote him further which is a sense of the timeless as well as of the temporal together, is what makes a writer traditional. And it is at the same time what makes a writer most acutely conscious of his place in time, of his own contemporaneity."[2]

On the basis of the above observation, it seems reasonable to maintain a point of view that Waugh's whole corpus of writing embodies his individual talent which feeds on the resources of the past tradition of fiction-writing on the one hand and envisages a perspective about the future. The emotion of art, to quote T.S. Eliot again is impersonal, and it is on the grounds of this contention that one has to judge the mind and art of Evelyn Waugh. His sense and sensibility are rich and fertile enough to grasp the impersonal significance of the actions and interests of the men and women living in society who form the nucleus of his imagination and motivate him to present the illusion of reality he finds himself confronted with. This impersonal attitude of Waugh's to the life and art of his time, in spite of his being so much sentimental and splenetic as he often does appear to be as a man to his reader, helps him most in becoming a ratiocinative artist of his time. Thus having freed himself from his emotions he continually seems to be surrendering himself as a man as well as an artist to something which is always more valuable and meaningful than what appears to him from the outside. The process of employing his razor-sharp intellect makes him treat his theme successfully in a depersonalised manner which helps him most in understanding and appreciating the spirit of his time. His mind appears to be a bit of finely filiated platinum which in itself remains quite unchanged and unaffected even if the two gases, namely oxygen and sulphuric acid are in the forms of tradition and individual talent mixed in its presence. The implication is the presence of the mind of a catalyst in him which simply observes without being affected by the object he sees. This attempt of his is found to have been started by him right from the earliest phase of his writing. In the mind of Evelyn Waugh as such one could easily trace the seeds of a catalyst who seems to be working with full care and caution from the earliest phase of his career. At the time of *Brideshead Revisited* (1945) one may have felt a lot of surprise and wonder at the sudden jerk of his sensibility but that might be dismissed as a passing phase in the progress of an artist who has to undergo a lot of self-sacrifice in course of writing. Waugh is as it appears a case of a 'continual extinction of personality' if this term of T.S. Eliot is deemed appropriate enough to bring out the full sense and meaning of his mind and art.

It must be mentioned here that his writings bear the impressions of a high-brow culture or a man who comes of a high strata of society. The reflections of such a sort of mind are discernible in the pages of his novels. Judged in the light of this observation he seems to be a man having developed a bias against the development of modern culture, but his reflections and reactions towards it carry a sufficient weight of his acute sensibility. There is little doubt that he satirises the achievements of the modern man and society; but very often his remarks seem to be just, forthright and mature. It may be thus remarked at the end of the assessment of his mind and art that Waugh appears to be a man of high-brow culture who has got a fine background of art and culture guiding him uninterruptedly. He is not an upstart talking frivolously about art and culture; there is a tone of modesty coupled with his wit and honour which magnify his mind and art all the more successfully in the eyes of scholars and critics. Moreover, it is not so easy to digest his thoughts and ideas which outwardly look flippant and platitudinous to an average mind but they bear the acute wisdom and insight of Evelyn Waugh in all its varieties.

Waugh as a novelist is a writer writing his time between the two world wars but he seldom appears to be reacting to it in a frenzied manner. His reactions are the reactions of an unruffled mind making a voyage within and without both giving vent to them in the world of his fiction. His approach as a writer is generally that of a classicist who endeavours to find out meaning and purpose in every walk of human life but there is something of a Romantic in his rebellion against the unnatural human society. Waugh is a clever artist who ingeniously chooses the eighteenth century mode of fiction-writing without making much ado about any novel trend of technique. Perhaps he may not be upheld as an innovator like Virginia Woolf or James Joyce. He is much more interested in his ideas and in conveying them with utmost sincerity and seriousness than in exploring possibilities of a new technique. In this, he would appear to belong to an older tradition—the tradition of the Naturalists. Surely, he has made a mark as a social reformer, a ratiocinative artist ruminating all the time over the provocative questions of the day and a futurist envisaging the shape of things to come. In other words, he impresses us as a rare phenomenon in the history of modern fiction who seems to be following a lonely path in the world of fiction; but he is very much in kinship with the tastes and attitudes of his readers whom he seldom overlooks. It is in keeping with their tastes and attitudes that he writes his novel keeping in his view the society he is writing for. It is not an attempt on the part of an artist for the sake of art, which, however, is not to accuse him of any inertness to form. He remains an impressive figure among the moderns—one with a profound sense of purpose, a clear vision and, above all, the determination of an artist to render all this into his works of art.

NOTES

1. The novelist at the Cross Roads and other essays on fiction and Criticism, David Lodge. Routledge and Kegan Paul, London, 1971, p. 18.
2. Tradition and Individual talent. Selected Essays by T.S. Eliot. London. Faber and Faber Ltd., 1951, p. 14.

Select Bibliography

Alldritt, Keith, *The Making of George Orwell an Essay in Literary History*.

Allen, Walter, *Tradition and Dream*, Phoenix House, London, 1964.

——, *The English Novel: A Short Critical History*, Penguin Book, 1970.

——, *Reading a Novel*, J.M. Dent & Sons Ltd., London, 1969.

Allott, Miriam, *Novelists on the Novel*, Third Impression, Routledge and Kegan Paul Ltd., 1960.

Allsop, Kenneth, *The Angry Decade—A Survey of the Cultural Revolt of the Nineteen-fifties*, Peter Owen Ltd., London Mcm LVIII, 1958.

Anthony Burgess, *The Novel Today*.

Baker, E.A., *The History of the English Novel*, Vol. 10, London, 1939.

Bergonzi, Bernard, *The Situation of the Novel*, Macmillan, 1970.

Bradbury, Malcolm, *Evelyn Waugh*, Edinburgh and London, 1964.

Brunton, Paul, *Spritual Crisis*.

Burgess, Anthony, *The Comedy of Ultimate Truths*, An article published in the spectator, April 15, 1966. Evelyn Waugh 1903-1966.

Carens, James F., *The Satiric Art of Evelyn Waugh*, University of Washington Press, Seattle and London.

Church, Richard, *The Growth of the English Novel.*

Churchill, Thomas, *The Trouble with Brideshead,* Modern Language Quarterly, 1967.

Churchill, W.S., *The Second World War*, 6 Vols., London, 1948-54, I Vol., London, 1959.

——, *The World Crisis 1911-18*, 6 Vols. London 1923-31, I Vol., London, 1931.

Connolly, Cyrill Vernon, *The Unquiet Grave*, 1961.

Cormic, Mc., *Catastrophe and Imagination.* An Introduction of the Recent English and American Novel, Longmans, Green and Co., London, New York, Toronto, 1957.

Corr, Patricia, Evelyn Waugh, *Sanity and* Catholicism, The Spectator, Autumn, 1962.

Daiches, David, *The Present Age*, Current Press, London, 1958.

——, *Critical Approaches to Literatures*, Longmans and Green & Co., London, New York, Toronto.

——, *The Novel and the Modern World* (rev. ed. Cambridge, 1960).

De Vitis, A.A., *Roman Holiday, the Catholic Novels of Evelyn Waugh*, Vision Press Ltd., 1958.

Donaldson, Frances, *Evelyn Waugh: Portrait of a Country Neighbour*, Printed in Great Britain, London, 1967.

Eliot, T.S., *Selected Essays*, London. Faber and Faber Ltd., 1951.

Ellman, Richard, and Fedelson, JR, *The Modern Tradition Backgrounds of Modern Literature*, New York, Oxford University Press, 1965.

Empson, William, *Seven Types of Ambiguity*, 1942.

Eugene Current Garcia, Walton R. Patrick, Scott, *Foresman and Co. Realism and Romanticism in Fiction.* An approach to the Novel. "Notes on the Decline of Naturalism".

Feinberg, Leonard, *The Satirist—His Temperament, Motivation and Influence*, 1963.

Fielding, Gabriel, *Evelyn Waugh: The Price of Satire,* The Listener Oct. 8, 1964.

Ford, Boris, *The Modern Age* (The Pelican guide to English life), Vol. 7, 1961.

Forster, E.M., *Abinger Harvest,* A Penguin Book, 1936.

——, *Aspects of the Novel*, London, 1927.

Gindin, James, *Post War British Fiction: New Accents and Attitudes*, Cambridge University Press, 1962.

Grant and Temperley, *Europe in the Nineteenth and Twentieth Centuries,* Longmans, Sixth edition Nov. 1964.

Hale, Nancy, *The Realities of Fiction*, London, Macmillan and Co. Ltd., 1963.

Hall, James, *The Tragic Comedians,* Seven Modern British Novelists.

Hollis, Christopher, *Evelyn Waugh*, Printed in Great Britain by F. Mildner and Sons, London, Longman Group Ltd., 1971.

Holroyd, *Emergence from Chaos.*

Hough, Graham, *The Total Dream,* The Muse and her chain III, The Listener, May 7, 1962.

——, *The Dark Sun,* A study of D.H. Lawrence.

J. Becker, George, *Modern Literary Realism,* Princeton and New Jersey, Princeton University Press, 1973.

James, Henry, *House of Fiction*, London, Rupert Hart Davis, 1957.

James, R.A. Scott, *Fifty Years of English Literature: 1900-1950,* 2nd Edition, 1956.

John, St. John, "Temporary Officers and Gentlemen", *An article published in the Sunday Times*, Sept. 7, 1969.

Karl, Frederick Robert, *A Reader's Guide to Great Twentieth Century English Novels.*

Kerman, Alvin B., *The Yale Review*—"The Wall and the Jungle". The early novels of Evelyn Waugh.

Kettle, Arnold, *An Introduction to the Novel*, Vol. II, 1962. Hutchinson University Library, London.

Killog Robert and Scholes Robert, "Plot in Narrative", *Perspectives on Fiction*. New York Oxford University Press, London, Toronto, 1968.

Lawrence, D.H., *Kangaroo.*

——, *Letter to Edward Garnett* (5 June, 1914) Letters (1932).

Leavis, F.R., *The Common Pursuit* (London, 1933).

——, *Fiction and the Reading Public* (London, 1932).

——, *New Bearings in English Poetry*, Rev. ed. London, 1950, Penguin, 1963.

Lidell, Robert, *Some Principles of Fiction*, Jonathan Cape, Thirty Bedford Square, London, 1956.

Lodge, David, *Language of Fiction,* Essays in criticism and verbal analysis of the English Novel.

——, *The* Novel*ist at the Crossroads and Other Essays on Fiction and Criticism*. Routledge and Kegan Paul, London, 1971.

Lubbock, Percy, *Craft of Fiction*, Jonathan Cape, Thirty Bedford Square London, 1960.

Maugham, W.S. *Ten Novels and Their Authors*, Penguin Book, 1969.

Mowat, Charles Loch, *Britain between the Wars 1918-1940,* Methuen & Co. Ltd., pp. 201-02.

Mucke, DC, *Irony*, Methuen & Co. Ltd., 1970, Printed in Great Britain.

O'Faolain, Sean, *The Vanishing Hero*, Studies in Novelists of the twenties, Eyre and Spittis Woode, London, 1956.

Pinto, V. de Sola, *Crisis in Modern Poetry,* 1880-1940.

Pollard, Arthur, *Satire*, Methuen & Co. Ltd., London.

Polts, L.J., *Comedy,* Hutchinson University Library, London.

Powell, Anthony, *Evelyns Diary*, London Magazine, August/ Sept. 1973.

Raban, Jonathan, *The Novel and the 1960s.*

Ratcliff, A.J.J., *Prologoue to Prose of Our Times.*

Raymond, Williams, *Culture and Society.*

Read, Herbert, *Essays on Literary Criticism*, Faber and Faber Ltd., London, 1967.

Richards, I.A., *Principles of Literary Criticism*, London, 1924.

——, *Practical Criticism: A Study of Literary Judgement*, London, 1929.

Routh, H.V., *English Literature and Ideas in the Twentieth Century*, Methuen & Co. Ltd., London (1950).

Rubin, Robinovitz, *The Reaction Against Experiment in English Novel.*

Russell, Bettrand, *New Hopes for a Changing World*, Allen and Unwin, 1960.

Sampson, George, *The Concise Cambridge History of English Literature*. 3rd Edition, 1972.

Schorer, Mark, *Modern British Fiction.*

Shaw, Margaret R.B., *Laurence Sterne, The Making of a Humorist, 1713-1762*, London, The Richards Press, Royal Opera Arcade, Pall Mall, 1957.

Stopp, Frederick, J., *Evelyn Waugh: Portrait of an Artist.* London, Chapman and Hall, 1958.

Styam, J.L., *The Dark Comedy,* Cambridge, At the University Press, 1968.

Toynbee, Arnold, *Civilization on Trial.*

Trevelyan, George Macaulay, *English Social History,* 1942.

Trilling, Lionel, *The Liberal Imagination*, 1961.

Turnell, Martin, *The Novel in France,* 1950.

Ward, A.C., *Twentieth Century Literature*, Methuen & Co. Ltd., 1963.

Warren, Austin and Welleck, Rene, *Theory of Literature.*

Wain, John, *Essays on Literature and Ideas*, London, Macmillan and Co. Ltd., New York, St. Martin Press, 1963.

Waugh, Alec, *My Brother Evelyn and other Profiles Cassell,* London, 2nd Edition, Jan. 1968.

Waugh, Evelyn, *A Little Learning, The First Volume of an Autobiography,* 1964.

——, *When the Going was Good.*

——, *Vile Bodies.*

——, *Work Suspended*, Penguin Series, 1963.

——, *Put Out More Flags.*

——, *Officers and Gentlemen.*

——, *Love Among the Ruins.*

——, *The Ordeal of Gilbert Pinfold.*

——, *Life of Ronald Knox.*

——, *Edmund Campion.*

Woolf, Virginia, *Modern Fiction,* The Common Reader, London, 1951, Hogarth Press.